SpringerBriefs in Psychology

SpringerBriefs in Behavioral Criminology

Series Editor

Vincent B. Van Hasselt
Department of Clinical and School Psychology
Nova Southeastern University
Fort Lauderdale, FL, USA

Behavioral Criminology is a multidisciplinary approach that draws on behavioral research for the application of behavioral theories and methods to assessment, prevention, and intervention efforts directed toward violent crime and criminal behavior. Disciplines relevant to this field are criminology; criminal justice (law enforcement and corrections); forensic, correctional, and clinical psychology and psychiatry: neuropsychology, neurobiology, conflict and dispute resolution; sociology, and epidemiology. Areas of study and application include, but are not limited to: specific crimes and perpetrators (e.g., homicide and sex crimes, crimes against children, child exploitation, domestic, school, and workplace violence), topics of current national and international interest and concern (e.g., terrorism and counter terrorism, cyber crime), and strategies geared toward evaluation, identification, and interdiction with regard to criminal acts (e.g., hostage negotiation, criminal investigative analysis, threat and risk assessment). The aim of the proposed Briefs is to provide practitioners and researchers with information, data, and current best practices on important and timely topics in Behavioral Criminology. Each Brief will include a review of relevant research in the area, original data, implications of findings, case illustrations (where relevant), and recommendations for directions that future efforts might take.

Monty T. Baker • Alyssa R. Ojeda
Hannah Pressley • Jessica Blalock
Riki Ann Martinez • Brian A. Moore
Vincent B. Van Hasselt

Violence in the Military

Springer

Monty T. Baker
College of Psychology
Nova Southeastern University
Fort Lauderdale, FL, USA

Alyssa R. Ojeda
College of Psychology
Nova Southeastern University
Fort Lauderdale, FL, USA

Hannah Pressley
College of Psychology
Nova Southeastern University
Fort Lauderdale, FL, USA

Jessica Blalock
College of Psychology
Nova Southeastern University
Fort Lauderdale, FL, USA

Riki Ann Martinez
College of Psychology
Nova Southeastern University
Fort Lauderdale, FL, USA

Brian A. Moore
Kennesaw State University
Kennesaw, GA, USA

Vincent B. Van Hasselt
Department of Clinical and School Psychology
Nova Southeastern University
Fort Lauderdale, FL, USA

ISSN 2192-8363 ISSN 2192-8371 (electronic)
SpringerBriefs in Psychology
ISSN 2194-1866 ISSN 2194-1874 (electronic)
SpringerBriefs in Behavioral Criminology
ISBN 978-3-031-26882-3 ISBN 978-3-031-26883-0 (eBook)
https://doi.org/10.1007/978-3-031-26883-0

This Springer imprint is published by the registered company Springer Nature Switzerland AG
The registered company address is: Gewerbestrasse 11, 6330 Cham, Switzerland

Preface

The global war on terrorism resulted in a continual involvement of the US military and allied nations from 2001 to 2021. While the training and experiences of service members are essential to national security, 20 years of conflict and ongoing military operations greatly impacted service members, families, and veterans. This impact is not unique to the US military but also extends to many of our close allies including Canada, the United Kingdom, Australia, and New Zealand. Standardized training, such as initial entry training, and specialized training, such as advanced schools for combat operations, develop the service member to withstand intense physical conditions and instill in them the courage to fight despite an oncoming danger. This training necessitates the need for a structure that contains and employs organized violence in an effective, efficient way. For this brief, violence is defined as behavior directed toward the self or others with the intent to injure or kill. The proponents of organized violence, such as military function, individual warfighters, and organizational structure, have changed as national threats evolve. The US military and supporting organizations are expected to deploy rapidly with extensive capabilities to address issues ranging from armed conflict to national emergencies. The requirement and expectation of constant readiness for or exposure to organized violence may contribute to the expression of violence outside of the military through the exacerbation of aggressive traits. This in turn is likely to impact mental health. Nevertheless, each service member acts within the realm of factors contributing to their environment, genetics, health, and experience. This comprehensive review addresses the impact of the aforementioned training and experiences on service members' mental health, behavior, and propensity toward non-combat-related violence. Non-combat-related violence manifests in a variety of ways, including suicidality and self-harm, sexual violence, intimate partner and domestic violence, and other violent criminal behaviors. Factors contributing to the perpetration of violence include personality traits (i.e., aggression), the military life cycle, interpersonal dynamics, and mental health. Each of the violence subtypes and contributing factors will be explored in this review. Violence in military populations can result in emotional, interpersonal, legal, and financial consequences for service members and their families. Additionally, the effects of military life on the propensity for violence do not dissipate when an individual leaves military service. Thus, identifying and addressing violent behavior and the factors enabling or exacerbating it is crucial for the long-term health and safety of service members, their families, and the communities in which they live.

Fort Lauderdale, FL, USA	Monty T. Baker
Fort Lauderdale, FL, USA	Alyssa R. Ojeda
Fort Lauderdale, FL, USA	Hannah Pressley
Fort Lauderdale, FL, USA	Jessica Blalock
Fort Lauderdale, FL, USA	Riki Ann Martinez
Kennesaw, GA, USA	Brian A. Moore
Fort Lauderdale, FL, USA	Vincent B. Van Hasselt

Acknowledgments

We want to extend a sincere thank you to our colleagues at Nova Southeastern University, Kennesaw State University, and University of Texas Health Sciences Center at San Antonio that enabled us to make this brief possible. The synergy of world-class military research teammates, military violence subject matter experts, and cutting-edge evidence-based training and treatment culminated in this in-depth review. A special thank you to all contributors for their willingness to dedicate months to synthesize the research in each of their respective chapters. To our service members, their families, veterans, and allies, we greatly appreciate all the sacrifices that are made every day to keep our world a safer place. Finally, thank you to all our family and friends that provided support and patience during this process. For all of us, violence in the military is a very important and personal topic and everyone contributed in their own way in order to complete this brief.

Contents

1 Introduction to Violence in the Military 1
References 2

2 Suicide and Self-Harm in the Military 3
2.1 Recent Suicide Statistics 4
2.1.1 Methods for Suicide 5
2.1.2 Known Concerns 6
2.2 The Interpersonal Theory of Suicide 6
2.2.1 IPTS Risk and Protective Factors 7
2.2.2 Military IPTS Research 7
2.3 Shame, Guilt, and Moral Injury 9
2.4 Other Mental Health Factors: Depression, Substance Use, Posttraumatic Stress Disorder, and Traumatic Brain Injury 11
2.5 Suicide Prevention Efforts 12
2.6 Summary 13
References 14

3 Military Sexual Violence: Sexual Assault, Sexual Harassment, and Sexual Hazing 19
3.1 Case Study 19
3.2 Military Sexual Trauma: Types of MST 20
3.2.1 Sexual Assault 20
3.2.2 Sexual Harassment 21
3.2.3 Sexual Hazing 21
3.3 Prevalence of Military Sexual Trauma 22
3.4 Reporting Procedures 23
3.4.1 Unrestricted Reporting 23
3.4.2 Restricted Reporting 24
3.4.3 Why Do Service Members Choose Not to Report? 24
3.5 Health Consequences of Military Sexual Trauma 25
3.5.1 Physical Health 25
3.5.2 Sexual Satisfaction 26

3.5.3 Mental Health. 26
3.6 Outcomes of Military Sexual Trauma 26
3.6.1 Survivor Outcomes 27
3.6.2 Abuser Outcomes. 29
3.7 Summary 29
References. 29

4 Intimate Partner and Domestic Violence Among Military Populations 33
4.1 Intimate Partner Violence and Domestic Violence. 33
4.2 Types of Maltreatment. 34
4.3 Intimate Partner Violence Recidivism and Escalation 34
4.4 Prevalence Among Military Populations 35
4.4.1 Reported Incidents 36
4.5 Context of Violence 39
4.6 Factors Associated with Military Service 40
4.7 Summary 42
References. 44

5 Violent Criminal Behavior in the Military 49
5.1 Risk Factors for Violent Crime 52
5.2 Factors Contributing to Violence 53
5.2.1 Aggression 53
5.2.2 Service-Related Factors 54
5.2.3 Mental Health. 58
5.3 Summary 67
References. 68

6 Clinical Implications, Limitations, Future Directions, and Conclusions 75
6.1 Clinical Implications 75
6.1.1 Suicide and Self-Harm in the Military. 75
6.1.2 Military Sexual Violence: Culture 76
6.1.3 Intimate Partner and Domestic Violence Among Military Populations. 78
6.1.4 Violent Criminal Behavior. 78
6.2 Limitations. 79
6.2.1 Suicide and Self-Harm in the Military. 79
6.2.2 Military Sexual Violence 80
6.2.3 Intimate Partner and Domestic Violence Among Military Populations. 80
6.2.4 Violent Criminal Behavior in the Military. 81
6.3 Future Directions 81
6.3.1 Suicide and Self-Harm in the Military. 81
6.3.2 Military Sexual Violence 82

6.3.3 Intimate Partner and Domestic Violence Among Military Populations. . . . 83
6.3.4 Violent Criminal Behavior in the Military. . . . 83
6.4 Conclusions 84
References. . . . 86

Index. . . . 89

About the Authors

Monty T. Baker, Ph.D. (Lieutenant Colonel, USAF, Ret.), received his Ph.D. in 2002 in Clinical Psychology at Nova Southeastern University. He completed his Clinical Psychology Residency at the Malcolm Grow Medical Center Andrews AFB, Maryland. Dr. Baker served over 30 years in the Military as an Operational and Clinical Psychologist with numerous combat deployments in support of OIF/OEF. He has also served as Military Primary Investigator on several grant-funded research studies and has over 160 academic presentations and publications. Dr. Baker is currently a POTFF Psychologist for U.S. Army Special Forces Underwater Operations Unit (SFUWO), Senior Advisor to the Military Psychology Group (MPG) at Nova Southeastern University, and Adjunct Professor at University of Texas-Health Science Center at San Antonio.

Alyssa R. Ojeda, M.S., is a fourth-year clinical psychology doctoral student at Nova Southeastern University and recipient of the two-year U.S. Army Health Professions Scholarship Program. She is the program coordinator of the Military Psychology Group within the First Responder Research and Training Team, led by Dr. Vincent Van Hasselt. Her research and clinical interests include resilience, post-traumatic growth, and the integration of physical activity for mental health prevention and intervention.

Hannah Pressley, MA, MS, is a fourth-year clinical psychology doctorate student at Nova Southeastern University. Prior to attending Nova, she earned a Master's degree in forensic and legal psychology at Marymount University. At present, she is active in the First Responder Research and Training Team throughout completing various projects, led by Dr. Vincent Van Hasselt. Hannah's primary research and clinical interests include health functioning of K9 handlers, neuropsychological evaluation and testing, and the clinical impact of military sexual trauma.

Jessica Blalock, M.S., is a fourth-year doctoral student in clinical psychology with a focus on first responders and forensic populations. She is an active member of the First Responder Research and Training Team and pioneered the largest survey of a national sample of first responders assessing occupational stress and mental well-being.

Riki Ann Martinez, MA, is a fourth-year clinical psychology doctoral student at Nova Southeastern University. She is currently the program coordinator of the Psychological Services for the Emotionally Distressed (PSED) clinic and works as a teacher's assistant for the Forensic Psychology Master's Program. Her clinical experiences consist of providing individual psychotherapy for individuals with serious mental illness and forensic populations. She also has significant experience conducting forensic evaluations for the court and working as a psychology trainee in a correctional facility. Her research interests include forensic assessment and criminal behavior and incarceration of military members.

Brian A. Moore, Ph.D., is an Assistant Professor of Psychology and the Director of the Center for the Advancement of Military and Emergency Services (AMES) Research at Kennesaw State University. Dr. Moore served 13 years in the Army and has extensively published on topics related to military and military-relevant populations.

Vincent B. Van Hasselt, PhD, is a Professor of psychology and Director of the Family Violence Program at Nova Southeastern University. He is also editor of *Aggression and Violent Behavior*: A Review Journal and *Journal of Family Violence*. Dr. Van Hasselt has served as Lecturer and Consultant to the FBI's Behavioral Science, Crisis Negotiation, and Law Enforcement Communication Units, and is part of the bureau's Crisis Prevention and Intervention Program. His clinical and research interests are in the areas of crisis and hostage negotiations, police stress and mental health, critical incident response, and the emerging field of behavioral criminology. Dr. Van Hasselt is also a certified police officer with the Plantation, Florida, Police Department.

Chapter 1
Introduction to Violence in the Military

The global war on terrorism resulted in a continual involvement of the United States military and allied nations from 2001 to 2021. Typically, only 10% of the active-duty force is deployed into combat (Bledsoe, 2022). However, service members require high-operational tempos to maintain training levels and occupational skill-sets. While the training and experiences of service members are essential to national security, 20 years of conflict and ongoing military operations greatly impacted both the service member and their families. This impact is not unique to the US military but also extends to many of our close allies including Canada, the United Kingdom, Australia, and New Zealand.

The purpose of the military is to provide organized violence as a solution to national threats (Thornhill, 2016). By entering such an organization, service members must prepare to be both the perpetrator and receiver of such violence. For this brief, violence is defined as behavior directed toward the self or others with the intent to injure or kill. Standardized training, such as initial entry training, and specialized training, such as advanced schools for combat operations, develop the service member to withstand intense physical conditions and instill in them the courage to fight despite an oncoming danger. This training necessitates the need for a structure that contains and employs organized violence in an effective, efficient way. The proponents of organized violence, such as military function, individual warfighters, and organizational structure, have changed as national threats evolve (Thornhill, 2016).

The US military and supporting organizations are expected to deploy rapidly with extensive capabilities to address issues ranging from armed conflict to national emergencies. Indeed, US forces are expected to withstand any threat to national security at any time, and thus, service members maintain constant training and vigilance. While the operational tempo of the US military has significantly decreased over the past few years, US forces maintain operational readiness through troop retention, training exercises, and training deployments to allied countries. This is also relevant for many service members in our allied counties.

M. T. Baker et al., *Violence in the Military*, SpringerBriefs in Psychology,
https://doi.org/10.1007/978-3-031-26883-0_1

The requirement and expectation of constant readiness for or exposure to organized violence may contribute to the expression of violence outside of the military through the exacerbation of aggressive traits. This in turn is likely to impact mental health. Nevertheless, each service member acts within the realm of factors contributing to their environment, genetics, health, and experience. This comprehensive review addresses the impact of the aforementioned training and experiences on service members' mental health, behavior, and propensity toward non-combat-related violence. Highlighting such issues provides military leaders insight into a broad range of behavioral, familial, and legal problems service members are facing and allows for change to be enacted to reduce the negative impact of warfighting on service members, their families, and citizens in the community. When possible, relevance to our allied countries will be discussed throughout the brief.

Non-combat-related violence manifests in a variety of ways, including suicidality and self-harm, sexual violence, intimate partner and domestic violence, and other violent criminal offenses. Factors contributing to the perpetration of violence include personality traits (i.e., aggression), the military life cycle, interpersonal dynamics, and mental health. Each of the violence subtypes and contributing factors will be explored in this review. Violence in military populations can result in emotional, interpersonal, legal, and financial consequences for service members and their families. Additionally, the effects of military life on the propensity for violence do not dissipate when an individual leaves military service. Of the 1869 veterans convicted of a federal crime in the 2019 fiscal year, 17.6% were convicted of violent crimes (United States Sentencing Commission, 2021). Thus, identifying and addressing violent behavior and the factors enabling or exacerbating it is crucial for the long-term health and safety of service members, their families, and the communities in which they live.

References

Bledsoe, E. (2022). *Answering: What percentage of military sees combat?*. The Soldiers Projects. https://www.thesoldiersproject.org/what-percentage-of-the-military-sees-combat/

Thornhill, P. G. (2016). *The crisis within: America's military and the struggle between the overseas and guardian paradigms*. RAND Corporation-Project Air Force.

United States Sentencing Commission. (2021). *Federal offenders who served in the armed forces*. https://www.ussc.gov/sites/default/files/pdf/research-and-publications/research-publications/2021/20211028_armed-forces.pdf

Chapter 2
Suicide and Self-Harm in the Military

Suicide is the most prevalent form of non-combat-related violence among US service members. Suicide is defined as, "death caused by self-directed injurious behavior with any intent to die as a result of the behavior" (Crosby et al., 2011). Suicide is the tenth leading cause of death in the United States across demographics and the second leading cause of death for individuals between the ages of 10 and 34 (National Institute of Mental Health, 2022).

The entry process to the US military requires that an individual is in good physical and psychological health, which might indicate that service members have a higher resiliency level than the general US population. Yet, US service members have been afflicted with consistently elevated rates of suicide deaths and suicidal behavior over the past two decades (Kang et al., 2015). By 2009, suicide rates within the military exceeded rates among the general US population, particularly for Whites and females (Reger et al., 2018b). Conversely, suicide trends in allied countries such as Canada and the United Kingdom do not reflect such trends. Suicide rates among the regular Canadian Armed Forces have not significantly increased over the past two decades and reflect patterns seen in their general populations (Boulos, 2021). Since the 1990s, the regular armed forces of the United Kingdom saw a decrease in suicides per year, and rates remained consistently lower than that of the general population. Notably, suicide rates within the UK military and the general male population have increased over the past 5 years (Ministry of Defence, 2020).

Considering this, we note that suicide in the US military has substantial impacts on the social, familial, and financial wellness of military members, community, and organizational readiness. Additionally, high suicide rates have significant implications for the mission readiness of the military. Rising suicide rates have prompted the Department of Defense and Congressional leaders to initiate an investigation into causes of suicidal behavior and factors that prevent it. Additionally, the service components have been provided resources to develop programs intended to bolster health and resilience in US service members (Department of Defense [DoD], 2022).

M. T. Baker et al., *Violence in the Military*, SpringerBriefs in Psychology,
https://doi.org/10.1007/978-3-031-26883-0_2

Despite these efforts, suicide remains a significant problem within the US military. Following the report of the most recent DoD suicide statistics (DoD, 2021), this chapter aims to provide insight into research investigating relevant theories and other contributing factors of suicidal behavior within the US military, such as Thomas Joiner's interpersonal theory of suicide (Joiner, 2005), the role of self-conscious emotions in suicide, and mental illness. Clinical implications and future directions for research are then proposed for the enhancement of suicide prevention and mental health treatment in the military.

2.1 Recent Suicide Statistics

In 2019, 344 active-duty service members, 65 reserve service members, and 89 national guard members died by suicide, with suicide mortality rates of 25.9, 18.2, and 20.3 per 100,000 service members, respectively (DoD, 2021). Across components, demographic features with higher suicide mortality rates include men, White/Caucasian and Asian/Pacific Islander race, non-Hispanic ethnicity, ages 20–24, enlisted, and divorced and never-married individuals. Ground combat occupations (e.g., infantry, gun crews, seamanship specialists) and electrical/mechanical equipment repairers both had the highest suicide mortality rate, each with 18.2 per 100,000. Interestingly, 56.1% of service members who died by suicide in 2019 had never deployed (DoD, 2021). Unfortunately, suicide mortality rates across all active duty and reserve branches have increased per year since 2011 (DoD, 2011). The national guard suicide mortality rate typically increases similarly to the active and reserve components; however, the national guard suicide mortality rate appeared to be drastically lower in 2019 than in previous years. In US veterans, the sex- and age-adjusted mortality rate was 26.9 per 100,000 in 2019 and was highest among males aged 18–34 (United States Department of Veterans Affairs, 2021). It is important to note that the increase in suicide mortality rates in US military members is comparable to that in the general US population, while suicide mortality rates in US veterans exceed those of the general US population.

A suicide attempt is defined as "A non-fatal self-directed potentially injurious behavior with any intent to die as a result of the behavior" (Crosby et al., 2011). In 2019, 1462 suicide attempts were reported among 1388 individuals, some of whom attempted suicide more than once (DoD, 2021). Demographic features of service members who attempted suicide were similar to those who died by suicide; however, almost all minority demographic groups had an increased proportion of suicide attempts. For example, 8.5% of service members who died by suicide in 2019 were female, while 31% of service members who attempted suicide were female. In 2019, enlisted personnel composed 97% of suicide attempts among active-duty service members. The most common occupational groups of service members who attempted suicide were electrical/mechanical equipment repairers (21.1%) among enlisted personnel and tactical operations officers (0.8%) and healthcare officers (0.7%) among commissioned officers. Seventy-two percent of service members who attempted suicide in 2019 had never deployed (DoD, 2021).

Demographic variables of suicide risk have been well established in both civilian and military populations (Schafer et al., 2021; Steele et al., 2018). A comprehensive meta-analysis of suicide risk factors in military members found that gender and race were not associated with suicide behavior in active-duty service members; however, service members were found to be at lower risk for suicidal behavior as they age. This is contrary to suicide risk trends in civilian populations, in which older Caucasian males are at the highest risk of suicide behavior (Conwell et al., 2002). While a small percentage of the total active-duty military force identifies as American Indian or Alaskan Native, suicide behavior is disproportionately higher in service members belonging to these two racial groups (O'Keefe & Reger, 2017).

Several studies have produced mixed results regarding the impact of deployment on suicide risk; however, most studies indicate a *lack* of or small association between deployment and suicide (Bryan et al., 2015). A report from Canadian forces examined members and identified a lack of association between deployment and suicide (Boulos, 2021). Additionally, methodological issues with deployment and suicide research and suggest that killing and witnessing death in combat specifically may be stronger predictive risk factors than "deployment" generally (Reger et al., 2018a, b). Finally, an epidemiological study found that combat deployment was not associated with suicide risk among veterans (Kang et al., 2015). Limited research has been conducted on deployed service members; however, what is known is that in severe cases (i.e., service members who received psychiatric aeromedical evacuation) service members who demonstrate suicidal behavior were more likely to be female, persons of color, in the Air Force, and serving in combat support or combat service support roles (Straud et al., 2020). Notably, a study using a large sample of psychiatric hospitalizations indicated that service members were five times more likely to die by suicide than service members with no psychiatric hospitalization, with the risk highest within 30 days after hospital discharge (Luxton et al., 2013). Among veterans, Bullman et al. (2018) found that veterans had a 56% increased risk of suicide after separation from the military compared to the general US population. The risk of suicide decreased as veterans' time since military separation increased, with suicide risk highest within 1 year of separation from the military. This may indicate identity dissonance concerns (Moore et al., 2022) and a point for future interventions and social support-building activities. Regardless, increased understanding of the demographic characteristics and predictors of suicide behavior in US service members and veterans is important, but only one piece of a complex, nuanced picture.

2.1.1 Methods for Suicide

Personally owned firearms are the most common method of completed suicide among active-duty military service members, comprising 59.9% of suicides (DoD, 2021). Similarly, firearms comprised 69.2% of suicide deaths among veterans (U.S. Department of Veteran Affairs, 2021). Among suicide attempts, drug/alcohol overdose is the most common method, comprising 53.1% of suicide attempts. Other known methods include a military-issued firearm, hanging/asphyxiation, poison, and trauma. Suicide methods in the UK military differed slightly in that 56% of completed suicides resulted from hanging, strangulation, or suffocation, while only 17% of suicides utilized firearms or explosives (Ministry of Defence, 2020). These differences likely reflect a cultural ubiquity, rather than intent to complete the suicide.

2.1.2 *Known Concerns*

Ten percent of US service members who died by suicide had a history of self-harm, and 43.6% had a mental health diagnosis, most commonly mood disorder, anxiety disorder, or substance use disorder. Similarly, Canadian Armed Forces reported mental health diagnoses of depressive, anxiety, posttraumatic stress, and other trauma or stress-related disorders as the most prevalent among those who completed suicide (Boulos, 2021). Of US service members with past suicide attempts, 30.1% had a history of self-harm, and 57.3% had a mental health diagnosis, most commonly mood, anxiety, or adjustment disorder (DoD, 2021). Lastly, 52.4% of active-duty service members who died by suicide and 61.7% of active-duty service members who attempted suicide in 2019 sought medical treatment within 90 days before their death or attempt. Specifically, 32% of service members who died by suicide and 47.2% of suicide attempters sought mental health treatment. Service members who died by or attempted suicide were likely to have relationship problems, legal/administrative involvement, or work stressors within 90 days of their death (DoD, 2021).

2.2 The Interpersonal Theory of Suicide

The interpersonal theory of suicide (IPTS; Joiner, 2005; Van Orden et al., 2010) has become widely accepted in suicide research and clinical practice. IPTS posits that three distinct characteristics separate those who die or nearly die by suicide from those who do not: thwarted belongingness, perceived burdensomeness, and acquired capability for suicide. Thwarted belongingness transcends temporary feelings of being left out or feeling alone and refers to the absence of meaningful, mutually supportive relationships. Perceived burdensomeness suggests the presence of relationships; however, an individual may feel their *self* is an unworthy, problematic liability to others, and that others would be better off without them. The theory explicitly notes that these views are often unfounded, and it is the *perception* of burdensomeness that can escalate an individual to contemplate and ultimately attempt suicide (Van Orden et al., 2010). Together, thwarted belongingness and perceived burdensomeness result in the desire for suicide, which can vary in intensity. Hopelessness about these two constructs—the perception that one will always be alone and a burden—is hypothesized to mediate the relationship between passive and active suicidal ideation (Van Orden et al., 2010).

Indeed, the high prevalence of suicidal ideation and low incidence of suicide suggests that the desire for suicide alone does not motivate an individual to complete suicide. Humans are evolutionarily programmed to fear and avoid threats to survivability; thus, an individual must *acquire* the ability to overcome this basic human process to complete suicide. The IPTS suggests this acquisition of capability for suicide consists of both reduced fear of death and increased physical pain tolerance, which are developed by habituation through repeated exposure to fear-inducing and physically painful experiences (Van Orden et al., 2010). Such experiences can include abuse, combat exposure, previous suicide attempts and self-harm, and even reckless activities one might engage in through genetically impulsive behavior. In summary, an individual must experience lasting feelings of isolation and perceived expendability while developing the ability to overcome our most basic survival instinct, to transition from suicidal desire to death by suicide.

2.2.1 IPTS Risk and Protective Factors

Unique factors contribute to the mitigation or exacerbation of risk factors described by IPTS among military personnel. For example, military values of camaraderie, honor, and duty can both enhance a sense of belongingness and increase susceptibility to feeling unworthy or self-contemptuous if an individual becomes afflicted by physical or psychological injury which interferes with their ability to serve their units or their families (Lusk et al., 2015; McCormick et al., 2019). Combat training and exposure to weapons and death may contribute to the capability for suicide; however, research investigating the impact of combat on suicidality is inconclusive. A meta-analysis investigating the association between deployment, combat experiences, and suicidal behavior found a small, positive effect between deployment and suicidality, with specific exposure to killing and war atrocities having the greatest effect on suicidal behavior in military personnel (Bryan et al., 2015). Notably, military personnel are more likely than civilians to have a history of childhood abuse (Blosnich et al., 2014) and sexual abuse (Schultz et al., 2006). The aforementioned exposure to painful experiences contributes to a generally higher capability of suicide and therefore greater risk of suicide attempt or completion among military personnel compared to civilians (Assavedo et al., 2018; Bryan et al., 2010).

2.2.2 Military IPTS Research

Research investigating IPTS constructs within the military has been variable; however, perceived belongingness and acquired capability for suicide are consistently shown to be significant factors influencing suicidal behavior in military personnel.

In a comprehensive study examining IPTS in a large sample of Army personnel, general hopelessness was strongly associated with suicidal thoughts, especially in those who also reported perceived burdensomeness (Chu et al., 2020). Interestingly, the capability for suicide predicted suicide attempts across military personnel but was not associated with suicidal thoughts, supporting the hypothesis that capability for suicide must be acquired to transition from suicidal ideation to suicide attempt (Van Orden et al., 2010). However, among military personnel who endorsed suicidal ideation, only perceived burdensomeness predicted suicide attempts (Chu et al., 2020).

Other literature supports perceived burdensomeness as the most pervasive construct of IPTS in military personnel. Among female veterans, those with a recent suicide attempt reported feelings of low self-worth and devaluation by others, whereas males with a recent suicide attempt were more likely to report feelings of frustration and failure (Denneson et al., 2020). In a study of female service members with a history of military sexual trauma (MST), fearlessness about death (i.e., capability for suicide) was most strongly associated with suicidal ideation, followed by perceived burdensomeness, after controlling for psychiatric symptoms and suicide attempt history. In the presence of fearlessness about death and perceived burdensomeness, thwarted belongingness was not associated with suicidal ideation (Monteith et al., 2017).

Similarly, in a study with treatment-seeking military personnel, the interaction between perceived burdensomeness and acquired capability was associated with suicidal behavior (Bryan et al., 2012). In samples of deployed military personnel seeking treatment for either mild traumatic brain injury or mental health problems, the relationship between acquired capability and suicidal behavior became stronger as perceived burdensomeness increased (Bryan et al., 2012). Again, thwarted belongingness was not associated with suicidal behavior in this sample of military personnel. It is worth noting this may be due to their status on active duty, whereas service members in the reserve components have fewer routine touchpoints with their unit's peers and leadership.

Indeed, in a cross-sectional study with a large sample of the National Guard members ($N = 934$), the three-way model of IPTS constructs was supported. The interaction of thwarted belongingness and perceived burdensomeness predicted suicidal ideation and resolved plans and preparations for suicide, while the three-way interaction including the acquired capability for suicide predicted lifetime suicide attempts (Anestis et al., 2015). Specifically, thwarted belongingness and perceived burdensomeness were positively related to lifetime suicide attempts at high levels of acquired capability and negatively related to lifetime suicide attempts at low levels of acquired capability. In other words, the acquired capability was an important component of the service member's transition between suicidal ideation and suicide attempt. Although context is important, presently, there is evidence that the IPTS can be useful in examining and predicting suicidal behavior in military personnel, with the strongest evidence for the impact of perceived burdensomeness and acquired capability on suicidal behavior. Additional research is required to enhance both the utility of the IPTS for predicting suicidal behavior as well as informing behavioral health treatment of at-risk military personnel.

2.3 Shame, Guilt, and Moral Injury

While the IPTS informs clinical understanding of suicide in the military, a deeper examination of other contributing factors is necessary to better predict and prevent suicidal behavior among military personnel. The direct examination of emotions related to suicidal behavior and attitudes is a crucial yet often overlooked part of suicide research. Specifically, shame and guilt are pervasive emotions among individuals engaging in suicidal ideation and behavior (Lester, 1998), yet little research exists to parse the effects of these emotions on suicidal behavior. While shame and guilt are both self-conscious emotions and frequently used interchangeably, they are indeed distinct, with a unique impact on an individual's mental health and behavior. Shame is defined as a negative emotion in which an individual self-evaluates their core being and believes they are flawed or do not meet a standard, resulting in feelings of worthlessness and powerlessness (Lewis, 1971; Tangney et al., 2007). Conversely, guilt stems from one's negative self-evaluation of their *behavior* rather than their *self* (Niedenthal et al., 1994; Tangney et al., 2007).

Factors of military service uniquely contribute to the development of shame and guilt compared to civilian populations. For example, the warrior ethos mentality (Riccio et al., 2004) held by military service members may contribute to feelings of failure or unworthiness in the presence of physical or psychological injury, thus evoking shame. Additionally, "combat-related guilt" has been identified as a construct resulting from acts of war perpetrated or witnessed by service members during deployment and has been shown to significantly impact service members' mental health (Marx et al., 2010). Shame and guilt are also highly associated with moral injury, an emerging and important risk factor for myriad social and psychological problems among military personnel (Griffin et al., 2019).

Military personnel who report suicidal ideation often endorse feelings of shame and guilt. Numerous studies report that shame and guilt exacerbate suicidal ideation, as well as other psychological symptoms including hopelessness, depression, and PTSD in a variety of service member presentations (Bryan et al., 2013a, b, c; Gaudet et al., 2016). The presence of shame and guilt has frequently been shown to mediate the effects of common psychological disorders previously thought to be directly associated with suicide ideation (Bryan et al., 2013a, b, c; Cunningham et al., 2019). Currently, there is a dearth of research investigating the relationships between shame, guilt, suicide attempt, and death by suicide. Notably, shame and guilt may contribute to the transition from passive to active suicidal ideation and suicide attempt through their impact on factors related to thwarted belongingness and perceived burdensomeness. For example, individuals experiencing shame often withdraw from others and may believe themselves unworthy of meaningful relationships (Tangney et al., 2007), thus increasing feelings of thwarted belongingness. Similarly, overwhelming guilt and remorse may invoke feelings of perceived burdensomeness. Research is needed to better understand the influence of shame and guilt on suicide attempts and death by suicide.

In recent years, moral injury has become a focus of current research among military personnel exposed to combat. Moral injury results when a service member commits "an act of transgression that severely and abruptly contradicts an individual's personal or shared expectation about the rules or code of conduct" (Litz et al., 2009). Indeed, Vermetten and Jetly (2018) discuss shame and guilt as the "pressure cookers" which exacerbate psychological disturbance and dysfunction commonly seen among service members struggling with moral injury. Aligned with this, Litz et al. (2009) propose a model which strongly integrates guilt and shame as both causal and consequential factors of moral injury. The impact of shame, guilt, and moral injury on suicidal behavior is an important area of exploration which can inform deeper understanding and enhance suicide prevention and intervention efforts for military personnel.

Since 2009, research investigating the effects of moral injury on suicidal behavior has proliferated. To understand the results of the first known study examining the relationship between moral injury and suicidal behavior, clarification of relevant terms is warranted. Bryan, Bryan et al. (2016) defined three distinct factors within moral injury: transgressions-self, transgressions-other, and betrayal. Transgressions-self occurs when an individual commits an act that violates their own moral beliefs, while transgressions-other occurs when an individual does not or cannot intervene when witnessing another commit an unjust or immoral act. Betrayal occurs when an individual feels misled, failed, or otherwise betrayed by a peer or leader. An initial study investigated the association between the three moral injury subscales on suicidal thoughts and behavior and found that both transgressions factors were reported significantly more among service members with prior suicide attempts compared to service members who endorsed suicidal ideation, suggesting service members struggling with incidents of transgression may be more motivated to transition from suicide ideation to attempt (Bryan et al., 2014). Additionally, transgressions-self was associated with more severe suicidal ideation, possibly due to the impact of shame and guilt related to self-committed immoral acts. Betrayal alone was not significantly associated with a suicide attempt or ideation but did influence the relationships between suicidal thoughts and behaviors and transgression factors. Continued research has supported these claims (Bryan et al., 2018; Levi-Belz & Zerach, 2018; Wisco et al., 2017; Zerach & Levi-Belz, 2018). Studies conducted among veterans have shown that the psychological impacts of moral injury persist long after service and continue to affect veteran health and well-being (Schumacher, 2017; Schwartz et al., 2021). Taken together, shame and guilt are found to significantly influence suicidal thoughts and behavior, particularly among those who struggle with committing or witnessing immoral acts during their service.

2.4 Other Mental Health Factors: Depression, Substance Use, Posttraumatic Stress Disorder, and Traumatic Brain Injury

Finally, a variety of mental diagnoses have been linked to suicidal ideation and behavior. Indeed, recent suicide statistics suggest that 43.6% of service members who die by suicide and 57.3% who attempt suicide have a mental health diagnosis—most commonly mood, anxiety, adjustment, or substance use disorder (DoD, 2021). A large study performing psychological autopsies of 135 Army suicide decedents found that 79.3% had a mental health diagnosis, with rates highest for depression, PTSD, alcohol abuse, and substance use disorder (Nock et al., 2017). A recent global meta-analysis[1] found the prevalence of depression to be higher in military populations than civilians and specifically among service members with alcohol and drug use concerns (Moradi et al., 2021). The meta-analysis reported global suicide attempt and suicide ideation prevalence to be 11%. Prevalence rates of suicide attempts were 30% among service members who endorsed substance use and 8% among service members who endorsed alcohol use. The prevalence rates of suicide ideation were 18% and 9% among these subgroups, respectively. Further, PTSD, alcohol use, and depression were the strongest predictors of suicide attempts among veterans, with comorbidity significantly increasing risk in veterans (Lee et al., 2018).

Posttraumatic stress disorder (PTSD) and traumatic brain injury (TBI) are common considerations examined in suicide research with military service members. Panagioti et al. (2012) conducted a meta-analysis to investigate the relationship between PTSD and suicidal behavior, identifying a strong, positive association between PTSD and suicidality across service member presentations and settings. This relationship was further strengthened by the presence of comorbid depression. In one of the only prospective studies known to date regarding suicide risk in service members, hyperarousal was found to be the only PTSD symptom cluster to significantly predict a subsequent suicide attempt, but only for combat-exposed service members (Stanley et al., 2019).

More recently, a meta-analysis conducted by McIntire et al. (2021) explored the relationship between TBI and suicidal behavior, as well as related contributing factors. Comorbid substance use disorder was found to significantly strengthen the association between TBI and suicide attempts, especially when symptoms of depression or PTSD were present. Further, comorbid TBI and PTSD as well as neurobiological considerations (i.e., enlarged thalamic volumes and fractional anisotropy) were also associated with higher rates of suicidal ideation. Repeated TBIs in particular (i.e., three or more lifetime TBIs) have been shown to increase the risk for suicidal behavior. Further, anger associated with brain injury can lead to the development of depression, which in turn heightens suicide ideation and risk for attempt in service members seeking outpatient care for mild TBI (Stanley et al.,

[1] Most studies were conducted with US military populations.

2017). While diagnoses are useful in the care of service members experiencing psychological distress, research highlights the utility of assessing and treating comorbidities and other factors that interact with mental diagnoses to change or strengthen their relationship to suicide ideation and attempt.

While current research suggests a clear link between various psychological disorders and suicidal behavior, it is important to consider the multitude of behavioral factors that contribute to suicidality. For example, Bryan et al. (2018) found that individuals with PTSD were more likely to endorse previous suicide attempts only if they also reported symptoms of moral injury. In other words, PTSD symptoms may not be enough to move an individual to transition from suicide ideation to attempt; however, feelings of shame, guilt, grief, and lack of self-forgiveness might. As research into mechanisms contributing to the relationship between mental health disorders and suicidality continues, psychological intervention can more accurately and effectively treat suicidal thoughts and behaviors, resulting in a happier, healthier population of military service members and a reduction in deaths by suicide.

2.5 Suicide Prevention Efforts

The US Department of Defense has implemented several strategies to combat psychological and behavioral sequelae of military service which have been found to contribute to suicidal behavior. Several organizations have joined the DoD in the fight against suicide at the federal, state, and community levels. Specifically, seven categories of prevention have been established by the DoD to address many contributory factors of suicide outlined in this chapter, and hundreds of programs have been implemented to bolster each. These categories include strengthening economic supports, strengthening access and delivery of suicide care, creating protective environments, promoting connectedness, teaching coping and problem-solving skills, identifying and supporting people at risk, and lessening harm and preventing future risk (Department of Defense, 2020). Given that firearms are the primary method of completed suicide among US military personnel, research into the association between firearm ownership, usage, and storage and suicide has proliferated in recent years.

A psychological autopsy of 135 Army suicide decedents between 2011 and 2013 found that firearm accessibility was associated with a significant increase in suicide risk and suggested modifying firearm access as an intervention target (Dempsey et al., 2019). Further, education about firearm safety and its connection with suicide prevention is effective in increasing firearm safety behaviors (Anestis et al., 2021b); however, it has been shown that military service members view firearm safety messaging as more credible when delivered by a military service member or law enforcement officer and find the messaging less credible when delivered by a healthcare provider (Anestis et al., 2021a, b). An inaugural national summit convened in June 2022 to specifically address the role that firearm safety, re-termed "lethal means safety (LMS)," plays in military suicide prevention (Betz et al., 2022).

Several recommendations were disseminated to facilitate the development of firearm-related research and intervention protocols.

In addition to LMS, other recent suicide prevention interventions have focused on increasing coping and stress management skills for younger and enlisted personnel, improving access to care, supporting military families, and thoroughly evaluating current and developing practices (DoD, 2020). While decades of research have targeted suicide prevention and intervention, suicide rates among the military and the general population continue to rise. Continued collaboration and efforts among researchers and behavioral health providers is crucial to deepen understanding of suicidal attitudes and behavior, improving detection and intervention, and ultimately saving hundreds of warfighter lives per year.

Augmenting these efforts, downtrace National Guard Bureau organizations and state veterans service agencies, for example, have partnered with the Substance Abuse and Mental Health Services Administration (SAMHSA) and the United States Department of Veterans Affairs (VA) to participate in the "Governors" and "Mayors" challenge—a suicide reduction initiative—focused on preventing suicide among service members, veterans, and their families. Key to these efforts is the implementation of suicide prevention coalitions. Once established, these groups operate as community-based initiatives that extend the reach of evidence-based prevention, intervention, and postvention resources and services to reach underserved communities and populations.

The objectives of these programs may include increasing the availability of suicide prevention gatekeeper trainings, decreasing perceived stigma of suicide, increasing awareness of suicide prevention and intervention strategies, increasing the use of evidence-based suicide prevention strategies, and collaborating with existing and/or emerging suicide prevention coalitions to achieve local objectives that contribute to large-scale positive outcomes.

2.6 Summary

This chapter reviewed the most recent suicide statistics within the US military, which remain elevated despite governmental, organizational, and community prevention efforts. Personal and organizational factors contributing to suicidal behavior in US service members, veterans, and our allies were explored including demographic and personality characteristics, interpersonal dynamics described in Joiner's interpersonal theory of suicide (Van Orden et al., 2010), emotional elements which may exacerbate suicidal behavior, and mental health symptoms and diagnoses. Current suicide prevention efforts were also discussed, focusing on recent DoD initiatives, firearm safety, and community-level organizations. The goal of this chapter was to provide an accurate picture of the current state of suicidal behavior within the US military, describe research which may inform future detection and prevention, and identify areas in which further research is warranted. Suggestions for clinical practice are discussed in the last chapter of the brief.

References

Anestis, M. D., Bond, A. E., Bryan, A. O., & Bryan, C. J. (2021a). An examination of preferred messengers on firearm safety for suicide prevention. *Preventive Medicine, 145*, 106452. https://doi.org/10.1016/j.ypmed.2021.106452

Anestis, M. D., Bryan, C. J., Capron, D. W., & Bryan, A. O. (2021b). Lethal means counseling, distribution of cable locks, and safe firearm storage practices among the Mississippi national guard: A factorial randomized controlled trial, 2018–2020. *American Journal of Public Health, 111*(2), 309–317. https://doi.org/10.2105/AJPH.2020.306019

Anestis, M. D., Khazem, L. R., Mohn, R. S., & Green, B. A. (2015). Testing the main hypotheses of the interpersonal–psychological theory of suicidal behavior in a large diverse sample of United States military personnel. *Comprehensive Psychiatry, 60*, 78–85. https://doi.org/10.1016/j.comppsych.2015.03.006

Assavedo, B. L., Green, B. A., & Anestis, M. D. (2018). Military personnel compared to multiple suicide attempters: Interpersonal theory of suicide constructs. *Death Studies, 42*(2), 123–129. https://doi.org/10.1080/07481187.2017.1334013

Betz, M. E., Stanley, I. H., Anestis, M. D., Bryan, C. J., Buck-Atkinson, J., Carey, N., et al. (2022). Firearm suicide prevention in the US military: Recommendations from a national summit. *Military Medicine*, usac371. https://doi.org/10.1093/milmed/usac371

Blosnich, J. R., Dichter, M. E., Cerulli, C., Batten, S. V., & Bossarte, R. M. (2014). Disparities in adverse childhood experiences among individuals with a history of military service. *JAMA Psychiatry, 71*(9), 1041–1048. https://doi.org/10.1001/jamapsychiatry.2014.724

Boulos, D. (2021). *2020 report on suicide mortality in the Canadian Armed Forces (1995 to 2019)*. https://www.canada.ca/en/department-national-defence/corporate/reports-publications/health/2020-report-on-suicide-mortality-in-the-caf-1995-to-2019.html

Bryan, A. O., Bryan, C. J., Morrow, C. E., Etienne, N., & Ray-Sannerud, B. (2014). Moral injury, suicidal ideation, and suicide attempts in a military sample. *Traumatology, 20*(3), 154. https://doi.org/10.1037/h0099852

Bryan, C. J., Bryan, A. O., Anestis, M. D., Anestis, J. C., Green, B. A., Etienne, N., et al. (2016). Measuring moral injury: Psychometric properties of the moral injury events scale in two military samples. *Assessment, 23*(5), 557–570. https://doi.org/10.1177/1073191115590855

Bryan, C. J., Bryan, A. O., Roberge, E., Leifker, F. R., & Rozek, D. C. (2018). Moral injury, posttraumatic stress disorder, and suicidal behavior among National Guard personnel. *Psychological Trauma: Theory, Research, Practice, and Policy, 10*(1), 36. https://doi.org/10.1037/tra0000290

Bryan, C. J., Clemans, T. A., & Hernandez, A. M. (2012). Perceived burdensomeness, fearlessness of death, and suicidality among deployed military personnel. *Personality and Individual Differences, 52*(3), 374–379. https://doi.org/10.1016/j.paid.2011.10.045

Bryan, C. J., Cukrowicz, K. C., West, C. L., & Morrow, C. E. (2010). Combat experience and the acquired capability for suicide. *Journal of Clinical Psychology, 66*(10), 1044–1056. https://doi.org/10.1002/jclp.20703

Bryan, C. J., Griffith, J. E., Pace, B. T., Hinkson, K., Bryan, A. O., Clemans, T. A., & Imel, Z. E. (2015). Combat exposure and risk for suicidal thoughts and behaviors among military personnel and veterans: A systematic review and meta-analysis. *Suicide and Life-threatening Behavior, 45*(5), 633–649. https://doi.org/10.1111/sltb.12163

Bryan, C. J., Morrow, C. E., Etienne, N., & Ray-Sannerud, B. (2013a). Guilt, shame, and suicidal ideation in a military outpatient clinical sample. *Depression and Anxiety, 30*(1), 55–60. https://doi.org/10.1002/da.22002

Bryan, C. J., Ray-Sannerud, B., Morrow, C. E., & Etienne, N. (2013b). Guilt is more strongly associated with suicidal ideation among military personnel with direct combat exposure. *Journal of Affective Disorders, 148*(1), 37–41. https://doi.org/10.1016/j.jad.2012.11.044

Bryan, C. J., Ray-Sannerud, B., Morrow, C. E., & Etienne, N. (2013c). Shame, pride, and suicidal ideation in a military clinical sample. *Journal of Affective Disorders, 147*(1–3), 212–216. https://doi.org/10.1016/j.jad.2012.11.006

Bullman, T., Schneiderman, A., & Bossarte, R. (2018). Suicide risk by unit component among veterans who served in Iraq or Afghanistan. *Archives of Suicide Research, 22*(1), 1–10. https://doi.org/10.1080/13811118.2017.1304308

Chu, C., Zuromski, K. L., Bernecker, S. L., Gutierrez, P. M., Joiner, T. E., Liu, H., et al. (2020). A test of the interpersonal theory of suicide in a large, representative, retrospective and prospective study: Results from the Army study to assess risk and resilience in Servicemembers (Army STARRS). *Behaviour Research and Therapy, 132*, 103688. https://doi.org/10.1016/j.brat.2020.103688

Conwell, Y., Duberstein, P. R., & Caine, E. D. (2002). Risk factors for suicide in later life. *Biological Psychiatry, 52*(3), 193–204. https://doi.org/10.1016/S0006-3223(02)01347-1

Crosby A. E., Ortega L., & Melanson C. (2011). *Self-directed violence surveillance: Uniform definitions and recommended data elements, version 1.0.* Centers for Disease Control and Prevention. https://www.cdc.gov/suicide/pdf/self-directed-violence-a.pdf

Cunningham, K. C., LoSavio, S. T., Dennis, P. A., Farmer, C., Clancy, C. P., Hertzberg, M. A., et al. (2019). Shame as a mediator between posttraumatic stress disorder symptoms and suicidal ideation among veterans. *Journal of Affective Disorders, 243*, 216–219. https://doi.org/10.1016/j.jad.2018.09.040

Denneson, L. M., Tompkins, K. J., McDonald, K. L., Hoffmire, C. A., Britton, P. C., Carlson, K. F., et al. (2020). Gender differences in the development of suicidal behavior among United States military veterans: A national qualitative study. *Social Science & Medicine, 260*, 113178. https://doi.org/10.1016/j.socscimed.2020.113178

Dempsey, C. L., Benedek, D. M., Zuromski, K. L., Riggs-Donovan, C., Ng, T. H. H., Nock, M. K., Kessler, R. C., & Ursano, R. J. (2019). Association of firearm ownership, use, accessibility, and storage practices with suicide risk among US Army soldiers. *JAMA Network Open, 2*(6), e195383. https://doi.org/10.1001/jamanetworkopen.2019.5383

Department of Defense. (2020). *Annual suicide report: Calendar year 2019.* https://www.dspo.mil/Portals/113/Documents/CY2019%20Suicide%20Report/DoD%20Calendar%20Year%20CY%202019%20Annual%20Suicide%20Report.pdf?ver=YOA4IZVcVA9mzwtsfdO5Ew%3d%3d

Department of Defense. (2021). *Suicide event report: The calendar year 2019 DoDESR annual report.* https://health.mil/Military-Health-Topics/Centers-of-Excellence/Psychological-Health-Center-of-Excellence/Department-of-Defense-Suicide-Event-Report

Department of Defense. (2022, March 22). *Memorandum for senior pentagon leadership commanders of the combatant commands defense agency and DoD field activity directors: Establishment of the suicide prevention response independent review committee.* https://media.defense.gov/2022/Mar/22/2002961288/-1/-1/0/ESTABLISHMENT-OF-THE-SUICIDE-PREVENTION-AND-RESPONSE-INDEPENDENT-REVIEW-COMMITTEE.PDF

Gaudet, C. M., Sowers, K. M., Nugent, W. R., & Boriskin, J. A. (2016). A review of PTSD and shame in military veterans. *Journal of Human Behavior in the Social Environment, 26*(1), 56–68. https://doi.org/10.1080/10911359.2015.1059168

Griffin, B. J., Purcell, N., Burkman, K., Litz, B. T., Bryan, C. J., Schmitz, M., et al. (2019). Moral injury: An integrative review. *Journal of Traumatic Stress, 32*(3), 350–362. https://doi.org/10.1002/jts.22362

Joiner, T. E. (2005). *Why people die by suicide*. Harvard University Press.

Kang, H. K., Bullman, T. A., Smolenski, D. J., Skopp, N. A., Gahm, G. A., & Reger, M. A. (2015). Suicide risk among 1.3 million veterans who were on active duty during the Iraq and Afghanistan wars. *Annals of Epidemiology, 25*(2), 96–100. https://doi.org/10.1016/j.annepidem.2014.11.020

Lee, D. J., Kearns, J. C., Wisco, B. E., Green, J. D., Gradus, J. L., Sloan, D. M., et al. (2018). A longitudinal study of risk factors for suicide attempts among operation enduring freedom and operation Iraqi freedom veterans. *Depression and Anxiety, 35*(7), 609–618. https://doi.org/10.1002/da.22736

Lester, D. (1998). The association of shame and guilt with suicidality. *The Journal of Social Psychology, 138*, 535–536.

Levi-Belz, Y., & Zerach, G. (2018). Moral injury, suicide ideation, and behavior among combat veterans: The mediating roles of entrapment and depression. *Psychiatry Research, 269*, 508–516. https://doi.org/10.1016/j.psychres.2018.08.105

Lewis, H. B. (1971). Shame and guilt in neurosis. *Psychoanalytic Review, 58*(3), 419–438.

Litz, B. T., Stein, N., Delaney, E., Lebowitz, L., Nash, W. P., Silva, C., & Maguen, S. (2009). Moral injury and moral repair in war veterans: A preliminary model and intervention strategy. *Clinical Psychology Review, 29*(8), 695–706. https://doi.org/10.1016/j.cpr.2009.07.003

Lusk, J., Brenner, L. A., Betthauser, L. M., Terrio, H., Scher, A. I., Schwab, K., & Poczwardowski, A. (2015). A qualitative study of potential suicide risk factors among Operation Iraqi Freedom/Operation Enduring Freedom soldiers returning to the continental United States (CONUS). *Journal of Clinical Psychology, 71*(9), 843–855. https://doi.org/10.1002/jclp.22164

Luxton, D. D., Trofimovich, L., & Clark, L. L. (2013). Suicide risk among US Service members after psychiatric hospitalization, 2001–2011. *Psychiatric Services, 64*(7), 626–629. https://doi.org/10.1176/appi.ps.201200413

Marx, B. P., Foley, K. M., Feinstein, B. A., Wolf, E. J., Kaloupek, D. G., & Keane, T. M. (2010). Combat-related guilt mediates the relations between exposure to combat-related abusive violence and psychiatric diagnoses. *Depression and Anxiety, 27*(3), 287–293. https://doi.org/10.1002/da.20659

McCormick, W. H., Currier, J. M., Isaak, S. L., Sims, B. M., Slagel, B. A., Carroll, T. D., et al. (2019). Military culture and post-military transitioning among veterans: A qualitative analysis. *Journal of Veterans Studies, 4*(2), 287–298.

McIntire, K. L., Crawford, K. M., Perrin, P. B., Sestak, J. L., Aman, K., Walter, L. A., et al. (2021). Factors increasing risk of suicide after traumatic brain injury: A state-of-the-science review of military and civilian studies. *Brain Injury, 35*(2), 151–163. https://doi.org/10.1080/02699052.2020.1861656

Ministry of Defence. (2020). *Suicides in the UK regular armed forces: Annual summary and trends over rime 1 January 1984 to 31 December 2019*. https://assets.publishing.service.gov.uk/government/uploads/system/uploads/attachment_data/file/880253/20200326_UK_AF_Suicide_National_Statistic_2020_O.pdf

Moore, B. A., Collette, T. L., & Judkins, J. L. (2022). Identity dissonance in recently separated military veterans. In R. Gurang (Ed.), *Routledge resources online: Psychology in the real world* (Vol. 1). Routledge.

Monteith, L. L., Bahraini, N. H., & Menefee, D. S. (2017). Perceived burdensomeness, thwarted belongingness, and fearlessness about death: Associations with suicidal ideation among female veterans exposed to military sexual trauma. *Journal of Clinical Psychology, 73*(12), 1655–1669. https://doi.org/10.1002/jclp.22462

Moradi, Y., Dowran, B., & Sepandi, M. (2021). The global prevalence of depression, suicide ideation, and attempts in the military forces: A systematic review and meta-analysis of cross sectional studies. *BMC Psychiatry, 21*(1), 1–31. https://doi.org/10.1186/s12888-021-03526-2

National Institute of Mental Health. (2022, March). *Suicide*. Retrieved March 24, 2022 from www.nimh.nih.gov/health/statistics/suicide

Niedenthal, P. M., Tangney, J. P., & Gavanski, I. (1994). "If only I weren't" versus "If only I hadn't": Distinguishing shame and guilt in conterfactual thinking. *Journal of Personality and Social Psychology, 67*(4), 585–595. https://doi.org/10.1037/0022-3514.67.4.585

Nock, M. K., Dempsey, C. L., Aliaga, P. A., Brent, D. A., Heeringa, S. G., Kessler, R. C., et al. (2017). Psychological autopsy study comparing suicide decedents, suicide ideators, and propensity score matched controls: Results from the study to assess risk and resilience in service members (Army STARRS). *Psychological Medicine, 47*(15), 2663–2674. https://doi.org/10.1017/S0033291717001179

O'Keefe, V. M., & Reger, G. M. (2017). Suicide among American Indian/Alaska native military service members and veterans. *Psychological Services, 14*(3), 289–294. https://doi.org/10.1037/ser0000117

Panagioti, M., Gooding, P. A., & Tarrier, N. (2012). A meta-analysis of the association between posttraumatic stress disorder and suicidality: The role of comorbid depression. *Comprehensive Psychiatry, 53*(7), 915–930. https://doi.org/10.1016/j.comppsych.2012.02.009

Reger, M. A., Smolenski, D. J., Skopp, N. A., Metzger-Abamukang, M. J., Kang, H. K., Bullman, T. A., & Gahm, G. A. (2018a). Suicides, homicides, accidents, and undetermined deaths in the US military: Comparisons to the US population and by military separation status. *Annals of Epidemiology, 28*(3), 139–146. https://doi.org/10.1016/j.annepidem.2017.12.008

Reger, M. A., Tucker, R. P., Carter, S. P., & Ammerman, B. A. (2018b). Military deployments and suicide: A critical examination. *Perspectives on Psychological Science, 13*(6), 688–699. https://doi.org/10.1177/1745691618785366

Riccio, G., Sullivan, R., Klein, G., Salter, M., & Kinnison, H. (2004). *Warrior ethos: Analysis of the concept and initial development of applications*. Wexford Group International Inc.

Schafer, K. M., Duffy, M., Kennedy, G., Stentz, L., Leon, J., Herrerias, G., et al. (2021). Suicidal ideation, suicide attempts, and suicide death among veterans and service members: A comprehensive meta-analysis of risk factors. *Military Psychology, 34*(2), 1–18. https://doi.org/10.1080/08995605.2021.1976544

Schumacher, W. M. (2017). *Moral injury and suicidal ideation after military service: Mediating and moderating factors* (Doctoral dissertation). University of Oregon.

Schultz, J. R., Bell, K. M., Naugle, A. E., & Polusny, M. A. (2006). Child sexual abuse and adulthood sexual assault among military veteran and civilian women. *Military Medicine, 171*(8), 723–728. https://doi.org/10.7205/MILMED.171.8.723

Schwartz, G., Halperin, E., & Levi-Belz, Y. (2021). Moral injury and suicide ideation among combat veterans: The role of trauma-related shame and collective hatred. *Journal of Interpersonal Violence*, NP13952. https://doi.org/10.1177/08862605211007932

Stanley, I. H., Joiner, T. E., & Bryan, C. J. (2017). Mild traumatic brain injury and suicide risk among a clinical sample of deployed military personnel: Evidence for a serial mediation model of anger and depression. *Journal of Psychiatric Research, 84*, 161–168. https://doi.org/10.1016/j.jpsychires.2016.10.004

Stanley, I. H., Rogers, M. L., Hanson, J. E., Gutierrez, P. M., & Joiner, T. E. (2019). PTSD symptom clusters and suicide attempts among high-risk military service members: A three-month prospective investigation. *Journal of Consulting and Clinical Psychology, 87*(1), 67–78. https://doi.org/10.1037/ccp0000350

Steele, I. H., Thrower, N., Noroian, P., & Saleh, F. M. (2018). Understanding suicide across the lifespan: A United States perspective of suicide risk factors, assessment & management. *Journal of Forensic Sciences, 63*(1), 162–171. https://doi.org/10.1111/1556-4029.13519

Straud, C. L., Moore, B. A., Hale, W. J., Baker, M., Gardner, C. L., Shinn, A. M., et al. (2020). Demographic and occupational risk factors associated with suicide-related aeromedical evacuation among deployed US military service members. *Military Medicine, 185*(11–12), e1968–e1976. https://doi.org/10.1093/milmed/usaa201

Tangney, J. P., Stuewig, J., & Mashek, D. J. (2007). Moral emotions and moral behavior. *Annual Review of Psychology, 58*, 345–372. https://doi.org/10.1146/annurev.psych.56.091103.070145

United States Department of Veterans Affairs. (2021). *National veteran suicide prevention: Annual report*. https://www.mentalhealth.va.gov/docs/data-sheets/2021/2021-National-Veteran-Suicide-Prevention-Annual-Report-FINAL-9-8-21.pdf

Van Orden, K. A., Witte, T. K., Cukrowicz, K. C., Braithwaite, S. R., Selby, E. A., & Joiner, T. E., Jr. (2010). The interpersonal theory of suicide. *Psychological Review, 117*(2), 575–600.

Vermetten, E., & Jetly, R. (2018). A critical outlook on combat-related PTSD: Review and case reports of guilt and shame as drivers for moral injury. *Military Behavioral Health, 6*(2), 156–164. https://doi.org/10.1080/21635781.2018.1459973

Wisco, B. E., Marx, B. P., May, C. L., Martini, B., Krystal, J. H., Southwick, S. M., & Pietrzak, R. H. (2017). Moral injury in U.S. combat veterans: Results from the National Health and Resilience in Veterans Study. *Depression and Anxiety, 34*(4), 340–347. https://doi.org/10.1002/da.22614

Zerach, G., & Levi-Belz, Y. (2018). Moral injury process and its psychological consequences among Israeli combat veterans. *Journal of Clinical Psychology, 74*(9), 1526–1544. https://doi.org/10.1002/jclp.22598

Chapter 3
Military Sexual Violence: Sexual Assault, Sexual Harassment, and Sexual Hazing

3.1 Case Study

Service Member Chavez attended a mandatory night out to celebrate the completion of basic training with her platoon. On her way back to her barracks, she ran into her commanding officer, Master Sergeant Jenkins, who ordered her to have sexual intercourse with him while she was under the influence of alcohol. Following the incident, Service Member Chavez had three options: (1) she could go to the medical emergency room immediately after the assault to report she had been sexually assaulted, (2) report her assault to her commanding officer, Master Sergeant Jenkins, or (3) make no report and stay silent about the incident. If she chose to report her assault, she would be faced with the decision to file as either Restricted or Unrestricted. By choosing Restricted Reporting, the case is filed as an "alleged assault," the survivor remains anonymous and receives medical attention and resources, and no charges are filed. In this situation, she and her abuser would remain in their respective positions with no administrative changes.

By choosing Unrestricted Reporting, an open formal investigation of the incident would commence, and both Service Member Chavez and her abuser would be subjected to investigation. If the Military Criminal Investigative Office decided against the charges, Service Member Chavez would remain in her position in the platoon under her abuser. Service Member Chavez may decide to change her station or transfer; however, this would require another disclosure and a formal request to her commanding officer asking to leave her assignment early. If the Military Criminal Investigative Office decided there was not enough evidence to pursue a criminal investigation, Master Sergeant Jenkins and Service Member Chavez would have the allegation on their record and would remain in the same positions. As this allegation would stay on her record, she would face difficulty with a transfer, ultimately leaving Service Member Chavez to remain under the command of her abuser. If Service Member Chavez continued to make claims about the abuse, her commanding officer

M. T. Baker et al., *Violence in the Military*, SpringerBriefs in Psychology,
https://doi.org/10.1007/978-3-031-26883-0_3

may require an evaluation to determine Service Member Chavez's mental and physical state. Depending on the outcome of the evaluation, Service Member Chavez may face two options: (1) discharge before the completion of her contract and receive dishonorable status or (2) stay in her current position and complete the requirements of her contract.[1]

This vignette provides only a brief glimpse into how a situation of military sexual trauma (MST) may unfold; it also highlights the complexities of sexual violence in the military setting. Service members are met with various obstacles unique to military culture that civilian survivors do not encounter. MST has intricacies that significantly impact the individual's likelihood of reporting; therefore, it is continuously underreported and untreated (Mengeling et al., 2014). These challenges are reflected in the current prevalence rates which inaccurately portray the true rate of occurrence.

As awareness grows, the military has updated policies on reporting and investigative processes; yet, some areas require more attention and advocacy. Currently, any sexual offense within the military has been termed military sexual trauma (MST). However, it must be noted that this term does not cover all types of sexual violence. MST is an umbrella term that does not fully encompass the sexual victimization that occurs in the military. For example, sexual hazing is far removed from the conversation. MST typically refers to the trauma experienced by an individual who has been sexually assaulted or harassed.

3.2 Military Sexual Trauma: Types of MST

3.2.1 Sexual Assault

Considering MST is the broad term used regarding sexual violence, it is pertinent to understand how the military defines each type of sexual trauma. The following section will provide the current definitions of various types of MST according to the updated policy set forth by the Department of Defense (DoD). According to the DoD Policy Brief No. 6495.01, sexual assault is characterized as follows:

> Intentional sexual contact [is] characterized by the use of force, threats, intimidation, or abuse of authority or when the victim does not or cannot consent. As used in this Instruction, the term includes a broad category of sexual offenses consisting of the following specific UCMJ offenses: rape, sexual assault, aggravated sexual contact, abusive sexual contact, forcible sodomy (forced oral or anal sex), or attempts to commit these offenses. (2021)

[1]This brief case vignette has been created to help the readers understand how average cases progress. It is factious but has been gathered from the author's observations working with victims of military sexual assault. Victims' stories read much like the case provided; however, no confidential information was used within the chapter.

3.2.2 Sexual Harassment

Sexual harassment has been widely accepted in the past as part of military culture and experience; however, as of 2022, sexual harassment has been deemed a crime in the military (Shane, 2022). To provide a standardized approach to sexual harassment reports, the US Army defines sexual harassment as follows:

> Sexual harassment as a form of gender discrimination which includes unwelcome sexual advances, requests for sexual favors and other verbal and or physical conduct of a sexual nature between the same or opposite genders when: (1) Submission to, or rejection of, such conduct is made explicitly or implicitly a term or condition of a person's job, pay or career. (2) Submission to, or rejection of, such conduct by a person is used as a basis for career or employment decisions affecting that person. (3) Such conduct has the purpose or effect of unreasonably interfering with an individual's work performance or creates an intimidating, hostile, or offensive working environment. (4) Any person in a supervisory or command position who uses or condones implicit or explicit sexual behavior to control, influence, or affect the career, pay, or job of personnel is engaging in sexual harassment. Similarly, anyone who makes deliberate or repeated unwelcome verbal comments, gestures, or physical contact of a sexual nature is engaging in sexual harassment. (United States Military Academy West Point, 2022)

While this definition provides continuity of reporting and consequences, there is a noteworthy gender difference in sexual harassment experiences that warrant mention. Wood and Toppelberg (2017) found men are subjected to harassment requiring them to prove their heterosexual, masculine nature, whereas women experience unwanted sexual comments and propositions from their colleagues.

3.2.3 Sexual Hazing

While not formally recognized as a form of MST, sexual hazing warrants mention as a form of sexual violence that occurs in the military. Researchers have recognized hazing as an informal socialization ritual that occurs as a rite of passage in the military setting (Hoyt et al., 2011; Pershing, 2006; Wood & Toppelberg, 2017). Hazing is utilized as a tool to indoctrinate individuals into the culture of the organization (Groah, 2005). Wood and Toppelberg (2017) conclude that sexualized hazing typically consists of sexual assault and sexual harassment, however, is completed with the intention of indoctrination. Albeit the act is the same, sexual hazing may be seen differently because it is viewed as a tradition that everyone must endure (Hoyt et al., 2011; Wood & Toppelberg, 2017). A dearth of literature exists on the implications, prevalence, and outcomes for servicemen and women that have experienced sexual hazing; however, limited research and anecdotal evidence suggest sexual hazing has negative implications on the mental well-being of service member survivors.

3.3 Prevalence of Military Sexual Trauma

In 2006, the US Congress passed a law requiring servicemen and women to complete a biannual survey to identify the prevalence of MST and provide adequate services for survivors (Sierra, 2021-present). The 2018 results of this survey indicate the prevalence of reported MST was approximately 13,000 servicewomen and an estimated 7500 servicemen. This equates to approximately 20,500 MST reports in 2 years. Annually, 6% of servicewomen are raped (Sierra, 2021-present). Countries such as Australia, New Zealand, Canada, and the United Kingdom also reported experiencing sexual violence within their military forces (Fisher, 2020; Lindeman, 2022; Morgan, 2020; Wyndham, 2020). In 2016, the New Zealand Defence Force noted 400 reports of sexual violence among their 14,000 personnel (Fisher, 2020). As this global phenomenon has impacted the military forces for decades, these numbers are likely an underestimation of overall prevalence. While these numbers are startling, they are not retroactive and do not include individuals who were previously victimized or sexual harassment/hazing cases.

Wide estimates of MST have been published in recent years. For example, researchers have estimated the prevalence rate for reports of sexual harassment and assault to be approximately 15.7%, including both military personnel and veterans (Wilson, 2018). Based on military diagnostic records, Collette et al. (2022) identified much lower comparative incidence rates of sexual abuse that required medical attention at 6 service members per 10,000. Further, reported experiences of MST are estimated to be 1 in 4 female veterans and 1 in 100 male veterans (Disabled American Veteran, 2022). In a meta-analysis of 69 studies that met inclusion criteria and were examined for current prevalence rates across different aspects of MST, Wilson (2018) observed that up to 13.9% of participants reported experiencing sexual assault and 31.9% experienced sexual harassment. Further, the researchers highlighted women as the primary victim of both sexual assault and sexual harassment. Another study reported that an estimated 21.6% of servicewomen and 6.6% of servicemen report sexual harassment (Wood & Toppelberg, 2017). Servicewomen who reported experiencing sexual harassment were 14 times more likely to experience sexual assault, whereas servicemen were 50 times more likely (Wood & Toppelberg, 2017). These findings are likely an estimate and could be explained by the disproportionate rates of disclosure between genders. Indeed, the recent epidemiologic study by Collette et al. (2022) examining active-duty military medical diagnoses made between 1997 and 2015 reported that service members who identified as female, Black, in the Army, between the ages of 20 and 24, and lower enlisted (i.e., E-1 to E-4) were overrepresented (relative to density) in medical care seeking for sexual abuse. It warrants mention that research in sexual hazing is largely nonexistent in the military literature, especially regarding reporting, prevalence, and resources. The majority of current research focuses on the prevalence of sexual assault, victim demographics, and victim outcomes.

Of note, MST rates have increased with the change in reporting standards and the current discussion about MST. Over the past decade, the military has made substantial steps to correct systematic challenges and injustices survivors of MST face. However, current procedures lack certain protections for the survivor, as evidenced in Service Member Chavez's narrative. To decrease the prevalence of MST and increase disclosure confidentiality, the US Army employed the Sexual Assault Response Coordinator (SARC) and Sexual Harassment Assault Response Prevention (SHARP). SARC and SHARP employees are separate assignments and do not typically overlap with other jobs on base. While there is some level of confidentiality provided when utilizing SARC/SHARP, they are new programs that are consistently changing and being updated. These response personnel are missioned to provide education and training to military personnel regarding preventing, identifying, and reporting instances of MST (My Army Benefits, 2021). In addition to this mandate, a SARC also provides survivors with resources and reporting options (DoD, 2021).

3.4 Reporting Procedures

Military personnel may underreport sexual violence for a variety of reasons. When considering sexual victimization within the military, it is critical to understand the differences in reporting options. Although these procedures were updated in November 2021, they do not encompass the extent of sexual trauma experienced and only explicitly include sexual assault or harassment. Currently, there are no reporting guidelines for sexual hazing. While the policy brief is quite extensive, it creates a multitude of challenges for survivors. At present, survivors are offered two options: (1) make a report through the appropriate chain of command or (2) file no report and remain silent about the abuse. Reporting options are detailed throughout the following section to provide a synthesized overview of current policies set forth by the DoD (2021). According to these policies, survivors of MST may choose to report their victimization in one of two manners: Unrestricted or Restricted (DoD, 2021).

3.4.1 Unrestricted Reporting

Unrestricted Reporting initiates an investigation, alerts command staff, and provides medical evaluation and treatment for the survivor (DoD, 2021; 32 CFR 105.8, 2016). While receiving medical care, the survivor will be assigned victim advocates both in SARC and SHARP. Resources are provided for the survivor once they have filed DD Form 2910 (see form at https://www.esd.whs.mil/Portals/54/Documents/DD/forms/dd/dd2910.pdf). Additionally, Unrestricted Reporting extends resources to survivors from victim services once they have completed relevant paperwork. Should a survivor choose to decline command or DoD law enforcement involvement, the survivor does not have access to these resources (DoD, 2021; 32 CFR 105.8, 2016). Further, once Unrestricted Reporting has been selected, the survivor may not change to Restricted Reporting, and a full investigation may take place regardless of the survivor's decision. Both parties, the survivor and alleged abuser, are investigated until culpability is determined.

3.4.2 Restricted Reporting

According to the DoD (2021), if the survivor decides on Restricted Reporting, no further investigation is warranted, and the assault is labeled "an alleged sexual assault." The survivor's name remains anonymous, thereby the individual has no complaint attached to them and their chain of command is not notified (United States Dept of Veterans Affairs, 2019). If needed, the individual is provided medical attention (United States Dept of Veterans Army, 2019). Further, they are provided SARC and SHARP assistance to provide resources and information on reporting options. Restricted Reporting is not permitted in some jurisdictions or if the survivor discloses the assault to a mandatory reporter. Additionally, Restricted Reporting allows the survivor to convert to Unrestricted Reporting at any time.

3.4.3 Why Do Service Members Choose Not to Report?

While there are two options for reporting MST, *unrestricted* and *restricted*, service members likely opt not to report. Mengeling et al. (2014) conducted a study to determine potential reasons survivors may not report. The researchers found servicewomen chose not to report due to actual and perceived consequences. Servicewomen with higher rank and more education chose to report incidents of MST at a higher frequency than those with lower rank and education level (Mengeling et al., 2014). Common considerations to refrain from reporting included potential career consequences, embarrassment, and lack of faith in the system. Although not statistically significant within the study, servicewomen also reported experiencing fear of reprisal, poor medical treatment, being ostracized by peers, and threats of collateral misconduct. This typically manifests in victims receiving citations for underage drinking or fraternizing at the time of the assault and receiving a mental health evaluation (Sierra, 2021-present). These mental health evaluations are being conducted inappropriately, as evidence indicates the survivor typically receives a diagnosis of personality disorder and is deemed unfit for service. This mechanism is a tactic used to quickly discharge the individual and prevent the allegations from taking place (Sierra, 2021- present).

Survivors of MST further endorsed feelings of discouragement from making a report, as 73% of service members that made reports experienced retaliation from their chain of command (Protect Our Defenders, 2021). Servicewomen who filed unrestricted reports disclosed experiencing a loss of confidentiality and negative career effects. Such consequences due to reporting MST has long been a threat to survivors of MST, which the DoD and US Senate are now publicly recognizing as an issue (Gilbred, 2017; Protect Our Defenders, 2021). With increasing debate, these departments have jointly attempted to remove the requirement to report to a commanding officer and demand immediate mental and physical health checks (Gilbred, 2017). With this attention, the DoD (2021) has made substantial changes to the reporting procedures in hopes of decreasing negative outcomes of reporting.

3.5 Health Consequences of Military Sexual Trauma

Various factors impact a service member's decision to report MST, and these factors are largely influenced by the outcomes and options provided to the survivors. Disclosing military sexual assault before 2006 was considered taboo as individuals experienced severe consequences for whistleblowing. With changes in laws, policies, and reporting procedures, survivors have been encouraged to speak out about their assault and are now provided various resources within the military including programs such as Sexual Harassment Assault Response and Prevention (SHARP) and Sexual Assault Response Center (SARC). These programs employ uniformed service members to provide awareness and advocacy, which is intended to create a stronger sense of unity, empathy, and validation for MST survivors. While the military is actively making changes to help the survivor, statistically, there has been no increase in reporting (Myers, 2017). The following section will provide current literature on the long-term physical and mental health risks associated with survivors of MST.

3.5.1 Physical Health

Research suggests MST survivors develop various physical health risks including chronic pain, pulmonary disease, and liver disease (Kimerling et al., 2016; Suris & Lind, 2008). Suris and Lind (2008) conducted a meta-analysis to examine the physical and psychological health of MST survivors. They found women were at the highest risk for developing negative health outcomes as a result of MST; however, men also experienced detrimental health impacts as a result. Women experienced overall poorer health and more chronic medical conditions, including obesity, substance use and abuse, and a more sedentary lifestyle, whereas men had higher rates of AIDS associated with MST (Suris & Lind, 2008). Further, Forkus et al. (2021) examined the association between MST experience and engaging in risky behaviors. They found individuals with MST experience had higher rates of substance use, disordered eating, suicidal behaviors, and overt sexual behavior (Forkus et al., 2021).

3.5.2 *Sexual Satisfaction*

Researchers examined female veterans' sexual satisfaction after experiencing MST (McCall-Hosenfeld et al., 2009) and found that female veterans with a history of MST reported lower levels of sexual satisfaction than those with no history of MST. Similarly, Pulverman et al. (2019) found that MST was associated with sexual dysfunction and lower sexual satisfaction. In consideration of this, McCall-Hosenfeld et al. (2009) theorized that women with a history of MST are predisposed to experiencing higher rates of interpersonal and occupational dissatisfaction and in turn, experience a lower quality of life.

3.5.3 *Mental Health*

To expand on the physical health outcomes previously discussed, Calhoun et al. (2018) examined the association between MST and mental health outcomes. They found both MST and combat exposure were positively correlated with posttraumatic stress disorder (PTSD) and depressive symptoms. Despite these mental health outcomes, servicewomen with a history of MST were no more likely than others to receive services from the Veterans Health Administration. This is particularly concerning as servicewomen experience higher rates of major depressive disorder and PTSD after experiencing MST, and survivors of sexual abuse report higher rates of sleep disturbances and chronic pain (Kelly et al., 2011).

When examining rates of suicidality in survivors of MST, Kimerling et al. (2016) found service members who reported MST were at an increased risk for suicidal behavior. Even after adjusting for various demographics (e.g., age, medical morbidity, mental health conditions), MST was a significant risk factor for suicide in both men and women (Kimerling et al., 2016). Further, they found that MST also increased the risk for alcohol and substance abuse. Holder et al. (2022) found veteran survivors of MST reported poorer overall psychological outcomes than civilian sexual assault survivors. Military survivors of MST indicated worse psychological outcomes and lower health satisfaction than civilian survivors (Holder et al., 2022). Current literature suggests MST survivors experience a variety of physical and mental health consequences that can cause long-term negative health outcomes.

3.6 Outcomes of Military Sexual Trauma

Research suggests that service members who have experienced MST reported high levels of trauma and posttraumatic stress symptoms resulting from the event. Factors that impacted and potentially exacerbated the trauma experienced included the abuser being a close friend or colleague, the use of a weapon, and the perception of inadequate response by the judicial system (McCall-Hosenfeld et al., 2009). With the complexities of the military environment, survivors and abusers experience different outcomes than the general population. The following section will discuss some potential outcomes specific to military personnel.

3.6.1 Survivor Outcomes

3.6.1.1 Revictimization

Wood and Toppelberg (2017) found that servicemen who experienced sexual hazing were significantly more likely than servicewomen to suffer multiple perpetrators. Researchers further concluded men report higher rates of sexual harassment from groups than from individuals. Forkus et al. (2021) found individuals with MST history were more likely to engage in risky sexual behaviors, had higher rates of sexually transmitted infections, and had higher rates of multiple assaults from multiple perpetrators. Additionally, Suris and Lind (2008) indicated individuals with a history of childhood sexual trauma were at a higher risk for revictimization, especially in the military setting. Various factors contributed to these findings; however, researchers indicated the two main moderators were military culture and the type of indoctrination that occurred for the service member within the military setting.

These factors remain unique to survivors of military sexual trauma as they are placed in a position to receive assistance in the same environment the traumatic event occurred. Military and civilian survivors may experience similar consequences such as hopelessness, blame, and mistreatment; however, military personnel may feel rejected by their peers, become accused of lying, or be deemed incompetent (Northcut & Kienow, 2014). These accusations serve as a form of revictimization and may cause similar physical and psychological outcomes as the assault itself. Studies support this finding indicating that the impact of military trauma is cumulative and compounding (Northcut & Kienow, 2014).

3.6.1.2 Loss of Identity

Becoming a member of the military requires a change in identity. Transitioning from civilian to soldier demands a level of commitment, honor, and ownership, all of which become imbued in the individuals' sense of self (Northcut & Kienow, 2014). After experiencing MST, military identification and identity can be tainted, therefore, causing a loss of identity both personally and professionally. This is unique to MST and does not typically occur in civilian sexual assault. Military personnel may challenge or resist their membership in the atmosphere that led to their traumatization, causing further distress, withdrawal, and isolation. Not only do they feel disconnected from their environment, but colleagues and peers may also exclude them, preventing any comradery or social support needed to process and cope with the experience (Northcut & Kienow, 2014; Schmid, 2010).

Additionally, a service member who reported their assault may lose their job or be transferred to another unit, further exacerbating their sense of loss and de-identification. Protect Our Defenders (2021) reported 67% of servicewomen who reported their assault faced some sort of retaliation. Further, one-third of service-women who reported were discharged from the military within a year of reporting (Protect Our Defenders, 2021). Not only do these harrowing statistics discourage service members from reporting, but it also reinforces their loss of identity. In situations where service members are discharged, they potentially face loss of benefits, access to post-service resources, and ostracization by their community resulting in reduced social support. This in turn may contribute to a post-service identity dissonance that prohibits the service member from fully engaging with their community (see Moore et al., 2022).

3.6.1.3 Extraneous Health Diagnosis

One mechanism for reporting requires the survivor to disclose their experience of sexual violence to a commanding officer or direct supervisor. The commanding officer may then decide what next steps are taken; the report can either be dismissed completely or filed as Unrestricted or Restricted (32 CFR 105.8, 2016). This system allows commanding officers accused of MST to require a mental or physical health evaluation of the service member claiming sexual assault, in an attempt to stifle the report attempt or retaliate against the survivor. Each reporting method has unique barriers for the survivors; however, any report results in immediate psychological and medical evaluation. These evaluations are often completed before the investigation begins (32 CFR 105.8, 2016).

Due to these practices, many service members receive unjust mental health diagnoses and are discharged from their service (Weener Moyer, 2021). For example, many veterans have received a diagnosis of a personality disorder after a claim of sexual violence. This diagnosis would be an essential piece to dishonorably discharge the service member, as it changes the individual's military eligibility and medical benefits (Northcut & Kienow, 2014; Protect Our Defenders, 2021; Sierra, 2021- present). With increased advocacy and awareness, this procedure has become less frequent. Myers (2017) reported military officers who were discharged with the provision of personality disorders are now eligible for an upgraded discharge and a change in diagnosis to posttraumatic stress disorder/military sexual trauma (PTSD/MST). This allowed survivors that reported MST and subsequently received a personality disorder diagnosis and discharge to obtain reprieve (Gilbred, 2017). While these changes were intended to encourage MST reporting, survivors appear to continue to remain hesitant to report assault or harassment for fear of retaliation.

3.6.2 *Abuser Outcomes*

Despite the increase in reporting and changes in policies, MST convictions may not have similarly increased. As of 2021, unrestricted reports had increased by over 23%, yet conviction rates had decreased by approximately 80% (Secretary of Defense, 2022). Protect Our Defenders (2021) found that 225 of 5640 were tried by court-martial, and of the 225 cases, only 50 abusers were convicted. These low conviction rates often leave survivors feeling defeated and distrustful of the military's judicial system. Additionally, the DoD Sexual Assault Program (2021) and prevention policy details the specific consequences of committing sexual abuse as follows:

> Punishment imposed, if any, including the sentencing by judicial or nonjudicial means, including incarceration, fines, restriction, and extra duty as a result of a military court martial, federal or local court, and other sentencing, or any other punishment imposed.

Weener Moyer (2021) reported very few convictions for MST occur in the military justice system and often take several years to achieve a final decision in court. Considering over 20,500 MST reports were made in 2019, and approximately 6% of servicewomen are raped annually, fewer than 1% of these cases result in conviction (Sierra, 2021-present). Nonprofit organizations, such as Protect Our Defenders, are working toward awareness and reform to allow survivors to seek justice for their abuse despite the barriers within the military culture.

3.7 Summary

Miliary sexual trauma (MST) is a pervasive issue throughout the US military. Definitions of types of MST (i.e., sexual assault, sexual harassment, and sexual hazing) were discussed along with prevalence rates. Survivors of military sexual violence face challenges unlike those in civilian life, including revictimization, difficulty reporting, repeated exposure to their abuser, and feelings of helplessness. These factors are unique to military culture due to the commitment to service, rank, and formality required in service. Health consequences and outcomes of MST in the military were examined in-depth. Continued research will help understand the continued challenges that emerge and how to best improve the treatment and evaluation of MST. The last chapter of the brief will address clinical implications, limitations, and future directions of military sexual violence.

References

32 CFR 105.8 – Reporting options and Sexual Assault Reporting Procedures. (2016). Retrieved from https://www.law.cornell.edu/cfr/text/32/105.8

Calhoun, P. S., Schry, A. R., Dennis, P. A., Wagner, H. R., Kimbrel, N. A., Bastian, L. A., Beckham, J. C., Kudler, H., & Straits-Tröster, K. (2018). The association between military sexual trauma and use of VA and non-VA health care services among female veterans with military service in Iraq or Afghanistan. *Journal of Interpersonal Violence, 33*(15), 2439–2464. https://doi.org/10.1177/0886260515625909

Collette, T. L., Esenwein, S. V., Sprague-Jones, J., Moore, K. E., & Sterling, E. (2022). Incidence rates of emotional, sexual, and physical abuse in active duty military service members, 1997–2015. *Aggression and Violent Behavior*. https://doi.org/10.1016/j.avb.2022.101745

Department of Defense. (2019, May 2). *DOD sexual assault prevention and response: What you need to know*. https://www.defense.gov/Explore/News/Article/Article/1831742/dod-sexual-assault-prevention-and-response-what-you-need-to-know/

Department of Defense. (2021, November). *Sexual assault prevention and response: Program procedures* (Policy Brief No. 6495.01). Department of Defense, United States of America. https://www.esd.whs.mil/Portals/54/Documents/DD/issuances/dodd/649501p.pdf

Disabled American Veteran. (2022, July 6). *Military sexual trauma – MST.* DAV. https://www.dav.org/veterans/resources/military-sexual-trauma-mst/#:~:text=How%20common%3F,What%20are%20the%20associated%20symptoms%3F

Fisher, D. (2020, July 15). New review finds a 'code of silence' problems dooming plan to eliminate sexual violence in our military. *New Zealand Herald*. https://www.nzherald.co.nz/nz/new-review-finds-a-code-of-silence-among-the-problems-dooming-plan-to-eliminate-sexual-violence-in-our-military/7AVTOA25GXOUAKLKKPBTHL5MUE/

Forkus, S. R., Weiss, N. H., Goncharenko, S., Mammay, J., Church, M., & Contractor, A. A. (2021). Military sexual trauma and risky behaviors: A review. *Trauma, Violence, & Abuse, 22*(4), 976–993. https://doi.org/10.1177/1524838019897338

Gilbred, K. (2017, July). *Challenging military sexual violence.* http://nlgmltf.org/military-law-library/publications/memos/military-sexual-violence/

Groah, J. S. (2005). *Treatment of fourth class midship- men: Hazing and its impact on academic and military performance; and psychological and physical health*. Naval Postgraduate School.

Holder, N., Maguen, S., Holliday, R., Vogt, D., Bernhard, P. A., Hoffmire, C. A., Blosnich, J. R., & Schneiderman, A. I. (2022). Psychosocial outcomes among veteran and non-veteran survivors of sexual assault. *Journal of Interpersonal Violence*, 1–23. https://doi.org/10.1177/08862605221090598

Hoyt, T., Klosterman Rielage, J., & Williams, J. F. (2011). Military sexual trauma in men: A review of reported rates. *Journal of Trauma & Dissociation, 12*(3), 244–260. https://doi.org/10.1080/15299732.2011.542612

Kelly, U., Skelton, K., Patel, M., & Bradley, B. (2011). More than military sexual trauma: Interpersonal violence, PTSD, and mental health in women veterans. *Research in Nursing & Health, 34*, 457–467. https://doi.org/10.1002/nur.20453

Kimerling, R., Makin-Byrd, K., Louzon, S., Ignacio, R. V., & McCarthy, J. F. (2016). Military sexual trauma and suicide mortality. *American Journal of Prevalent Medicine, 50*(6), 684–691. https://doi.org/10.1016/j.amepre.2015.10.019

Lindeman, T. (2022, June 1). Women in Canada's military face greater harm from comrades than enemy, says judge. *The Guardian*. https://www.theguardian.com/world/2022/jun/01/canadian-armed-forces-louise-arbour-report

McCall-Hosenfeld, J. S., Liebschutz, J. M., Spiro, A., & Seaver, M. R. (2009). Sexual assault in the military and its impact of sexual satisfaction in women veterans: A proposed model. *Journal of Women's Health, 18*(6), 901–909. https://doi.org/10.1089/jwh.2008.0987

Mengeling, M. A., Booth, B. M., Torner, J. C., & Salder, A. G. (2014). Reporting sexual assault in the military: Who reports and why most servicewomen don't. *American Journal of Preventative Medicine, 47*(1), 17–25. https://doi.org/10.1016/j.amepre.2014.03.001

Moore, B. A., Collette, T. L., & Judkins, J. L. (2022). Identity dissonance in recently separated military veterans. In R. Gurang (Ed.), *Routledge resources online: Psychology in the real world* (Vol. 1). Routledge.

Morgan, L. (2020). Understanding sexual offences in UK military and veteran populations: Delineating the offences and setting research priorities. *BMJ Military Health, 168*, 146–149. http://orcid.org/0000-0001-8422-9571

My Army Benefits. (2021, September 20). *Sexual harassment assault response and prevention (SHARP)*. https://myarmybenefits.us.army.mil/Benefit-Library/Federal-Benefits/SexualHarassment-Assault-Response-and-Prevention-(SHARP)?serv=122

Myers, M. (2017, August 07). *Former soldiers with service-connected sexual trauma can apply for discharge upgrades*. https://www.armytimes.com/news/your-army/2017/02/03/former-soldiers-with-service-connected-sexual-trauma-can-apply-for-discharge-upgrades/

Northcut, T. B., & Kienow, A. (2014). The trauma trifecta of military sexual trauma: A case study illustrating the integration of mind and body in clinical work with survivors of MST. *Clinical Social Work Journal, 42*(3), 247–259.

Pershing, J. L. (2006). Men and women's experiences with hazing in a male- dominated elite military institution. *Men and Masculinities, 8*(4), 470–492. https://doi.org/10.1177/1097184X05277411

Protect Our Defenders. (2021, May). *Facts on United States military sexual violence*. Protect Our Defenders. https://www.protectourdefenders.com/factsheet/.

Pulverman, C. S., Christy, A. Y., & Kelly, U. A. (2019). Military sexual trauma and sexual health in women veterans: A systematic review. *Sexual Medicine Reviews, 7*(3), 393–407. https://doi.org/10.1016/j.sxmr.2019.03.002

Schmid, M. N. (2010). Combating different enemy: Proposals to change the culture of sexual assault in the military. *Villanova Law Review, 55*(2), 475–508.

Secretary of Defense. (2022, February 15). *Actions to address and prevent sexual assault at military service academies*. United States Department of Defense. https://www.sapr.mil/sites/default/files/public/docs/reports/MSA/DoD_Actions_to_Address_Memorandum_to_the_Military_Departments_MSA_APY20-21.pdf

Shane, L. (2022, January 26). Sexual harassment in the military now a crime under Biden. *Military Times*. https://www.militarytimes.com/news/pentagon-congress/2022/01/26/sexual-harassment-in-the-military-now-a-crime-under-biden-order/

Sierra, G. (Host). (2021, September 30- present). *Sexual assault in the military* [Audio podcast]. Council on Foreign Relations. https://www.cfr.org/podcasts/sexual-assault-in-the-us-military

Suris, A., & Lind, L. (2008). Military sexual trauma: A review of prevalence and associated health consequences in veterans. *Trauma, Violence, & Abuse, 9*(4), 250–269. https://doi.org/10.1177/1524838008324419

United States Department of Veterans Affairs. (2019, January 7). *MST-related treatment and support resources for veterans*. https://www.mentalhealth.va.gov/msthome/treatment.asp

United States Military Academy West Point. (2022). *Sexual harassment*. https://www.westpoint.edu/about/west-point-staff/SHARP/sexual-harassment

Weener Moyer, M. (2021, October 11). 'A poison in the system': The epidemic of military sexual assault. *New York Times*. https://www.nytimes.com/2021/08/03/magazine/military-sexual-assault.html

Wilson, L. C. (2018). The prevalence of military sexual trauma: A meta-analysis. *Trauma, Violence, & Abuse, 19*(5), 584–597. https://doi.org/10.1177/1524838016683459

Wood, E. J., & Toppelberg, N. (2017). The persistence of sexual assault within the US military. *Journal of Peace Research, 54*(5), 620–633. https://doi.org/10.1177/0022343317720487

Wyndham, S. (2020, July 27). *Taking aim at military sexual violence*. The University of Sydney. https://www.sydney.edu.au/arts/news-and-events/news/2020/07/27/taking-aim-military-sexual-violence.html

Chapter 4
Intimate Partner and Domestic Violence Among Military Populations

4.1 Intimate Partner Violence and Domestic Violence

Domestic violence (DV) and intimate partner violence (IPV) are global health issues impacting civilian and military populations. Both terms describe similar dynamics and are often used interchangeably; however, there are important distinctions to be made between DV and IPV. In some jurisdictions, DV refers to any violence occurring within a household, irrespective of the familial relationship between the offender and victim, whereas IPV operationally defines the intimate nature of the relationship in which the violence occurs. The subtle distinction is IPV can occur regardless of whether those involved reside in the same household, while DV can occur in a household regardless of the relationship. More specifically, the term IPV is often used to describe acts of domestic violence, including "physical violence, sexual violence, stalking, and psychological aggression," perpetrated by a current or previous spouse or romantic partner (Kamarack et al., 2019, p. 5).

According to the Office of the Secretary of Defense (OSD, 2021), DV is defined as an offense involving the following:

> the use, attempted use, or threat use of force or violence against a person, or a violation of a lawful order issued for the protection of a person who is: a current or former spouse, a person with whom the abuser shares a child in common, or a current or former intimate partner with whom the abuser shares or has shared a common domicile; Person who is or has been in a social relationship of a romantic or intimate nature with the accused and determined to be an intimate partner. (p. 82)

More specifically, the OSD (2021) defines an intimate partner as a person

> who is or has been in a social relationship of a romantic or intimate nature with the alleged abuser, as determined by the length of the relationship, the type of relationship, and the frequency of interaction between the person and the alleged abuser. (p. 84)

According to DOD policy (DoDI 6400.06, 2007), domestic abuse, which consists of spouse and intimate partner abuse, is defined as "domestic violence, or a pattern of

M. T. Baker et al., *Violence in the Military*, SpringerBriefs in Psychology,
https://doi.org/10.1007/978-3-031-26883-0_4

behavior resulting in emotional/psychological abuse, economic control, and/or interference with personal liberty" (p. 35). Domestic violence is an offense under US Code, UCMJ, or State law "involving the use, attempted use, or threatened use of force or violence against a person, or a violation of a lawful order issued for the protection of a person" (p. 35). In addition, DOD policy specifies that domestic abuse must be directed toward, and domestic violence must be committed against, a person who is

> a current or former spouse; a person with whom the abuser shares a child in common; or a current or former intimate partner with whom the abuser shares or has shared a common domicile. (p. 35)

4.2 Types of Maltreatment

Per DoD policy (DoDM 6400.01, 2016), domestic abuse incidents are reported separately for four distinct types of abuse for either spouse or intimate partner abuse: "physical abuse, emotional abuse, sexual abuse, and neglect of spouse" (DoD, 2021, p. 39) (Table 4.1).

4.3 Intimate Partner Violence Recidivism and Escalation

IPV is a crime involving recidivism and escalation; perpetrators are often repeat abusers, and the severity of the violence usually intensifies over time (Hamrick and Owens, 2019). According to the Centers for Disease Control and Prevention (CDC), who collects IPV data on a national level, risk factors that can contribute to

Table 4.1 DOD definitions of types of maltreatment

Term	*Definition*
Physical abuse	The non-accidental use of physical force against a spouse or intimate partner that causes physical injury (e.g., bruise, cut, sprain, or broken bone) or reasonable potential for more than inconsequential physical injury
Emotional abuse	Non-accidental act or acts, excluding physical or sexual abuse, or threats adversely affecting the psychological Well-being of the partner (e.g., isolating partner from friends/family; restricting access to economic resources or benefits; threatening to harm the individual's children, pets, or property; or berating, disparaging, or humiliating the partner)
Sexual abuse	The use of physical force to compel the spouse or intimate partner to engage in a sexual act or sexual contact against his or her will, whether or not the sexual act or sexual contact is completed
Neglect of spouse	Withholding or threatening to withhold access to appropriate, medically indicated health care, nourishment, shelter, clothing, or hygiene where the spouse is incapable of self-care, and the abuser is able to provide care or access to care

Note. Reprinted from Kamarack et al. (2019)

IPV perpetration fall into four broad categories: individual (e.g., low self-esteem, anger, hostility, poor behavioral control, impulsivity), relational (e.g., relationship conflict involving jealousy, tension, possessiveness, families experiencing financial stress, association with aggressive peers), community (e.g., communities with high rates of crime and violence, low community involvement among residents, weak community sanctions against IPV), and societal (e.g., traditional gender roles, gender inequality, cultural norms supporting aggression, income inequality). Protective factors that minimize the risk of IPV perpetration include relationship factors (e.g., strong social support, stable and positive relationships) and community factors (e.g., resident involvement, coordinated resources and services, access to medical and mental health services) (see Appendix A for the full list of "CDC Risk and Protective Factors for IPV Perpetration"; CDC, 2021a, b).

Despite evidence indicating IPV is often underreported (Caetano et al., 2002; Emery, 2009; Chan, 2011), more than one in three women within the United States have experienced contact sexual violence (roughly 18.3%), physical violence (30.6%), and/or stalking (10.4%) by an intimate partner within their lifetime (CDC, 2021a, b; Smith et al., 2018). Additionally, over one-third of women have experienced psychological aggression by an intimate partner during their lifetime. According to these results from the National Intimate Partner and Sexual Violence Survey (NISVS) conducted in 2015, approximately one in four women and one in ten men experienced and reported IPV-related impact during their lifetime (Smith et al., 2018).

For victims, IPV can result in physical injury, mental health problems, and adverse maternal and neonatal pregnancy outcomes (e.g., neonatal death, preterm birth, and low birthweight; Alhusen et al., 2015). The residual symptoms of anxiety and stress continue to impact victims long after the incident(s) occur and result in 41% of women and 10% of male IPV victims experiencing symptoms of posttraumatic stress (D'Inverno et al., 2019). Among the most detrimental incidents, IPV can result in death (Marshall et al., 2005; Gierisch et al., 2013). Indeed, crime statistics indicate 16% of homicide victims in the United States are killed by an intimate partner. Among female homicide victims, in particular, nearly half are killed by a former or current male intimate partner (CDC, 2021a, b).

For perpetrators and specifically veterans, IPV can result in incarceration, as criminal offenses are both defined and prosecuted at the state-level. However, it should be noted that US federal law does also impose penalties on DV offenders (Sacco, 2015).

4.4 Prevalence Among Military Populations

Researchers continue to assess the prevalence and associated risk factors of IPV in the military. Most of the relevant literature pertains to experienced IPV among female veterans and IPV perpetrated by male veterans (Parr et al., 2021). As it relates to gender, IPV victimization is higher among women, and/or those with partners, in the military compared to the civilian population (Jones, 2012; Dichter et al., 2011). Utilizing the Defense Enrollment Eligibility Reporting Systems (DEERS) database, Campbell et al. (2003) concluded 30% of women reported IPV within their adult lifetime and 22% of women reported IPV during their military service. Additionally, women in the military have a greater reluctance than their civilian counterparts to report their victimization to authorities (House of Representatives Hearing, 2009a, b). Of female veterans who utilize Veterans Health Administration (VHA) primary care and were willing to participate in a survey, 18.5% reported sexual, psychological, or physical IPV within the past year (Kimerling et al., 2016). While not a direct comparison, the NISVS 2015 estimated 5.5% of women experienced contact with sexual violence, physical violence, and/or stalking by an intimate partner within the year preceding the survey (Smith et al., 2018).

Some research suggests physical violence is the most prevalent form of IPV in the military (Jones, 2012). A recent systematic review found the prevalence of physical IPV perpetrated in the past year by men in general military population samples ranged between 5.0% and 32.0% (Kwan et al., 2020) compared to studies in the general population with prevalence ranging from 4.0% to 15.0% (Whitaker, 2013; O'Leary et al., 2014; Okuda et al., 2015). Interestingly, the incidence of physical abuse that necessitated medical intervention in the active force is much lower than this, reported to be around 14 service members per 10,000 (Collette et al., 2022).

A recent study revealed that having a military connection significantly decreases the likelihood of reporting IPV compared to the civilian population. However, military status was found to not affect the likelihood to report robbery victimization. These results support the notion that military culture may reduce the probability that IPV-specific victimization will be reported to authorities compared to civilian counterparts (Becker & Bachman, 2019).

Pollard and Ferguson (2020) provided an international study highlighting a growing problem of IPV within military families. Researchers noted limited research into IPV perpetrated by Australian Defence Force (ADF) personnel or veterans. Thus, conducted an analysis to explore drivers that influence IPV occurrences by ADF personnel, and how the ADF enforces its zero-tolerance policy on domestic violence perpetration. Results revealed IPV perpetration by ADF personnel was attributed predominantly to problems within an individual rather than cultural or structural factors. Additionally, ADF members were reluctant to use ADF support services due to a perceived threat of medical downgrade or discharge from ADF service (Pollard & Ferguson, 2020).

4.4.1 Reported Incidents

Based on (FY) 2020 data of reported incidents to the DoD, there were 7903 "met criteria incidents" of domestic abuse. "Met criteria incidents" are reported incidents that have been presented to the Incident Determination Committee (IDC) and determined by a vote among IDC members to be either an act or failure to act according to standard policy (DoDI 6400.03, 2014; DoDM 6400.01, 2016). The met criteria incidents are then entered into the Central Registry in FY 2020. Of the total met criteria incidents of domestic abuse, physical abuse represented nearly three-quarters (73.11%), emotional abuse represented less than one-quarter (22.71%), and fewer involved sexual abuse (4.14%) and neglect (0.04%).

4.4.1.1 Spouse Abuse

Within the context of domestic violence, spousal abuse is evident and distinct from intimate partner abuse. A 2021 DoD report examining military abuse identified 12,663 incidents of spousal abuse reported involving currently married individuals. The report identified a spousal abuse rate of 204 per 1000 married military couples, which was a 6% decrease compared to the FY 2019 21.7% report rate. Of those reported, 6596 incidents met the criteria for spouse abuse. Per 1000 married military couples, the rate of spouse abuse incidents that met the criteria was 10.6%, which was a statistically significant 2.8% decrease compared to the FY 2019 10.9% rate. The spouse abuse victim rate was 8.6% per 1000 military couples, which was a 2.3% decrease compared to FY 2019 8.8% rate. Each of the decreases in rates was found to be statistically significant when compared to the 10-year average (DoD, 2021, p. 9).

Of the victims of spouse abuse incidents that met the criteria, 52% were service members and 48% were civilian spouses. In addition, 69% of victims were female and 31% were male. Overall, females experienced every type of abuse more than males. Among incidents of physical abuse, 65% of victims were female and 35% were male. For emotional abuse, 77% of victims were female and 23% were male. Spouse abuse victims who experienced sexual abuse were 94% female and 6% male. A total of 100% of victims of neglect were female; however, neglect accounted for less than 0.1% of the total met criteria for domestic abuse incidents (DoD, 2021, p. 45–46).

Of the perpetrators of spouse abuse incidents that met the criteria, 60% were service members and 40% were civilians. Regarding gender, 67% were male and 33% were female. Among male abusers, 2855 were service members, 596 were family members, and 11 were either contractors, non-beneficiaries, DoD civilians, or retired service members. Inversely, among female abusers, 373 were service members, 1521 were family members, and 15 were either contractors, non-beneficiaries, DoD civilians, or retired service members. Overall, the majority of abusers for every type of spouse abuse were male. For physical abuse, 63% of abusers were male and 37% were female. Among incidents of emotional abuse, 76% of abusers were male and 24% were female. Most spouse abusers of sexual abuse were male, 93% vs. 7% female. A total of 100% of abusers of neglect were male. Of abusers who were service members, 90% were male and 10% were female. In addition, the vast majority of service member abusers for sexual abuse, 99% vs. 1%, and emotional abuse, 93% vs. 7%, were male. Among service member abusers for physical abuse, 88% were male and 12% were female.

Regarding the pay grade of military spouse abusers, the majority were junior enlisted members. Specifically, 63% were E4-E6, 25% were E1-E3, and 7% were E7-E9. Five percent were officers, 3% were O1-O3, and 2% were O4-O10, and less than 1% were warrant officers (WO1-WO5). When compared to the FY 2020 total population of active-duty spouses, the differences among ratios of active-duty abusers by pay grade are pronounced. The ratio of active-duty spouse abusers is greater than the respective ratio of the total active-duty population of spouses in the E4-E6, 63% vs. 52%, and E1-E3, 24% vs. 8%, pay grades. Conversely, this ratio is less in the E7-E9, 7% vs. 17%; O1-O3, 3% vs. 10%; O4-O10, 2% vs. 11%; and WO1-WO5, 1% vs. 2%, pay grades (DoD, 2021, p. 46–54).

4.4.1.2 Intimate Partner Abuse

Intimate partner abuse can occur separately from spousal abuse when discussing domestic violence. In FY 2006, an intimate partner category was added to capture incidents of unmarried intimate partner abuse, whereby the abuser or the victim may have been a service member or civilian. In FY 2020, 2026 incidents were reported of intimate partner abuse. Of those reported, 1307 incidents met the criteria and involved 996 unique victims. Of the victims of intimate partner abuse, 68% were service members and 32% were civilians. Regarding gender, 74% were female and 26% were male (DoD, 2021, p. 55–57).

Of the met criteria for intimate partner abusers, 66% were service members and 34% were civilians. Regarding gender, 73% were male and 27% were female. Like those involved in spousal abuse, 59% of the military intimate partners who were abusers were junior enlisted members; roughly 59% were E4-E6 and 27% were E1-E3, 8% were E7-E9. Five percent were officers, 4% were O1-O3, and 1% were O4-O10, and 1% were warrant officers, WO1-WO5 (DoD, 2021, p. 58–60).

Rates of intimate partner abuse across the military are unable to be calculated, as the number of service members in intimate partner relationships as defined by the DoD is unavailable. However, the increases in the number of reported incidents, incidents that met criteria, and unique victims were all found to be statistically significant when compared to their respective 10-year averages (DoD, 2021, p. 10).

4.4.1.3 Adult Sexual Abuse

Within DV, sexual abuse is distinct from sexual assault. Contextually, it occurs within an intimate partner relationship or marriage as part of a larger behavioral pattern resulting in psychological abuse, financial control, or interference with personal autonomy. In FY 2020, 327 incidents of adult sexual abuse met the criteria and involved 303 unique victims, 94.4% of whom were female. Given more incidents were reported than victims, one or more victims experienced multiple incidents of sexual abuse. FY 2020 represented an increase of 17 met criteria incidents compared to FY 2019 (310) and was found to be statistically significant.

Among these victims, 53.8% were family members, 38.6% were service members, 7.6% fell into the "other" category, comprised of 6.9% non-beneficiaries, 0.7% DoD civilians, non-DoD civilians, government contractors, or retired service members. More specifically, 53.5% were female family members, 33.7% were female service members, and 7.2% fell into the "other" category. Males represented 5.6% of the victims of adult sexual abuse, whereby 4.5% were service members, 0.4% were family members, and 0.3% fell into the "other" category (DoD, 2021, p. 10; p. 61–64).

Of the 299 sexual abusers, 93.6% were male and 6.4% were female. Additionally, 80.9% were service members, 16.4% were family members, and 2.7% fell into the other category. Among the abusers who were service members, 98.3% were on active duty, and 1.7% were either in the Reserve or in the National Guard. The majority of service member abusers were enlisted members, 94.2%, and fewer were officers, 5.8% (DoD, 2021, p. 10; p. 61–64).

For two consecutive years, findings from the DoD report related to domestic abuse are mixed. While the rates of spousal abuse reports, met criteria incidents, and unique victims per 1000 married military couples decreased, the number of met criteria incidents and unique victims of intimate partner abuse increased. Despite a slight decrease in the ratio of adult sexual abuse incidents as a subgroup of DV in FY 2018, the ratio of sexual abuse incidents that met the criteria increased in FY 2020 when compared to the 10-year average. This increase contributes to an overall upward trend in adult sexual abuse incidents as a subset of domestic abuse over the last decade (DoD, 2021, p. 11).

4.4.1.4 Domestic Abuse Fatalities

In FY 2020, there were a total of 11 fatalities taken to the Incident Determination Committee (IDC) after the death of the victim that met the criteria for domestic abuse: 5 spouse abuse fatalities and 6 intimate partner abuse fatalities. Nine victims were female and two were male. Eight victims were active-duty members and three were civilians. Among the abusers, eight were male and three were female, six of whom were active-duty and five were civilians. Unfortunately, two of the victims and five of the abusers were previously known to the Central Registry due to their involvement in a previously met criteria of abuse (DoD, 2021, p. 65).

4.5 Context of Violence

Researchers acknowledge a need to move beyond descriptors of physical violence (e.g., severity and frequency) to make distinctions among types of IPV (Cook & Goodman, 2006; Johnson & Leone, 2005; Hardesty et al., 2015). Considering the context in which IPV occurs can determine the perpetrator's intent in their use of violence, the meaning of the violence to the victim, and the effect of the violence on the victim (Tinney & Gerlock, 2014). Johnson's (2010) typology of violence offers contextualized explanations of and differentiates between three main types of IPV: intimate terrorism, situational couple violence, and violent resistance. Distinctions among these types are based on identifying a pattern of coercive control.

Intimate terrorism is violence that occurs in the context of coercive control, with the repetitive use of violent and nonviolent tactics intended to maintain dominance over a partner's daily life (Johnson & Leone, 2005; Johnson, 2010; Johnson, 2017) and restriction of their liberties (Stark, 2009). The perpetual pattern of coercion and intimidation distinguishes this context and includes threats for noncompliance, surveillance of the victim's behavior, punishment, and attempts to diminish their resistance (Dutton & Goodman, 2005). Most often, these intimidation tactics are used to entrap the victim or narrow their contact with anyone other than the offender (Tinney & Gerlock, 2014). Coercive control can be described as personal and pervasive, whereby nonviolent tactics begin to take on violent meaning and instill fear (Stark, 2009).

Situational couple violence, formerly referred to as "common couple" or "situational" violence (Johnson, 2010), describes the violence that arises out of specific conflict (e.g., infidelity, finances) in the relationship that may escalate other issues (e.g., poor anger management, substance use). Within this context, the motive may be to control the situation but not the partner. While the frequency and severity of violence in situational couple violence is typically lower than in coercive controlling violence, it can still be dangerous, severe, and potentially result in injury and/or death (Johnson & Leone, 2005; Johnson, 2010; Johnson, 2017).

Violent resistance describes the violence that is used to fight back or defend oneself, for retaliation, to escape, as a last resort, or to an end (Johnson, 2010; Johnson, 2017). Generally, this is used by a victim who has been abused and battered over time as a strategy to stop the violence being perpetrated against them. The result of resistive violence can be as dangerous as IPV with coercive control and result in serious injury and/or death. However, it is qualitatively distinct in that it is a reaction to, rather than an expression of, coercive controlling violence (Tinney & Gerlock, 2014).

Another widely discussed construct as it relates to IPV is pathological violence, which may be influenced by mental health problems, traumatic brain injury, and/or substance use. It is important to note most individuals struggling with mental illness do not commit acts of violence, including IPV. Rather, mental illness, traumatic brain injuries, or substance abuse may serve as a co-occurring condition for perpetrators of IPV in any context of violence (Tinney & Gerlock, 2014).

4.6 Factors Associated with Military Service

Factors unique to military involvement likely exacerbate risks for perpetrators and victims of IPV (Kamarack et al., 2019). The lack of adjustment to specific sociodemographic factors may potentially impact the higher risk of IPV among military populations. For example, relative youth and male predominance and a greater risk of substantial alcohol consumption may increase IPV perpetration risk by military personnel (Wright et al., 2012; Fear et al., 2007). Indeed, just as violence has increased in some categories, so too has alcohol consumption (see Judkins et al., 2021). In a study examining alcohol dependence and abuse in 360,722 active-duty military personnel, Judkins et al. (2021) identified average incidence rates of 84.7 and 61.8 (respectively) per 10,000 service members between 2001 and 2018.

Service members and their families are subject to several social stressors, to include frequent relocation, which may influence relationship satisfaction and increase rates of IPV (Johnson et al., 2007). Among current-era female veterans, IPV has been associated with greater housing instability (Dichter et al., 2017). Difficulty coping with constant relocation atop other stressors related to military service (e.g., shift work, unpredictable deployments, reunification cycles) may contribute to relational instability or marital conflict and result in separation or divorce. Being separated from established support networks may increase stress in an intimate partnership and lead to feelings of social isolation. Particularly for those located overseas or at remote installations, there may be limited available options for victims to seek temporary safety or escape a potentially dangerous situation. Additionally, frequent relocation may impact nonmilitary spouses or partners' ability to maintain full employment. Lack of financial independence and the threat of reduced or lost military benefits may disincentivize victims of IPV to seek help (Kamarack et al., 2019). Finally, research has also indicated that prior interpersonal trauma may serve as a risk factor for IPV victimization or perpetration. Some data has suggested women with a history of childhood abuse may be more likely to join the military to escape a violent or unstable home environment (Gerber et al., 2014).

Military training may influence the use of violence as a method of conflict resolution (Jones, 2012) and result in an increased risk of IPV. Additionally, combat exposure has been associated with violence and offending (MacManus et al., 2013). Within the existing literature, there are conflicting results about the association between combat exposure and/or co-occurring combat-related conditions, including PTSD, TBI, substance use, and depression. For example, research has consistently supported the association between combat-related PTSD and IPV perpetration (Gerlock, 2004; Orcutt et al., 2003; Sayers et al., 2009; Taft et al., 2011). However, understanding the nature of the association between the two can be difficult to determine without accounting for previous IPV perpetration before deployment.

A recent study by Lane and colleagues examined the risk of violence by United Kingdom military personnel including relationship conflict and intimate partner violence (Lane et al., 2022). Researchers utilized data from personnel who had deployed to Iraq and/or Afghanistan ($N = 5437$). Results indicated 34.7% reported relationship conflict (arguing with partner) and 3.4% reported perpetrating physical IPV post-deployment, with males were more likely than females to report relationship conflict. There were similar rates of self-reported physical IPV perpetration among males and females. Building on a previous study (Kwan et al., 2020), results indicate deployment-related variables, mental health, and alcohol misuse problems were key factors associated with post-deployment relationship conflict and IPV (Lane et al., 2022).

Another study by Skomorovsky et al. (2015) explored the demands of military life (e.g., deployment) on family life. Researchers examined the effects of work-family conflict and marital satisfaction on intimate violence experienced by Canadian Armed Forces members ($N = 525$), and the impact of such violence on their psychological well-being. The results indicates that both work-family conflict and marital satisfaction were unique and significant predictors of emotional and physical violence experienced by Canadian Armed Forces members. Overall, the results point to the importance of examining the interrelationship between family stress and occupational stressors when exploring interpersonal violence and its psychological impact on military personnel (Skomorovsky et al., 2015).

There are also mitigating factors unique to military service. Access to healthcare, steady income and benefits, and family support services might alleviate financial stress and be a valuable early intervention target for at-risk partners. Any action taken to reduce personnel tempo (PERSTEMPO), such as limiting deployments, increasing time home between deployments, or fewer unaccompanied assignments, may help alleviate familial or interpersonal stress associated with departure and reintegration (Kamarack et al., 2019). Likewise, managing permanent change of station moves to increase time on station (Tong et al., 2018) may allow for social support networks and spousal employment to remain intact (Burke & Miller, 2016). Additionally, sanctions imposed at the discretion of military commanders, including administrative penalties or referrals for judicial action, may be more immediate and/or severe (e.g., reduced pay, loss of employment, and/or benefits) compared to civilian counterparts (Kamarack et al., 2019) (Table 4.2).

4.7 Summary

Domestic violence (DV) and intimate partner violence (IPV) are global health issues impacting both civilian and military populations. This chapter explored domestic violence and intimate partner violence impact among military populations. Definitions of DV and IVP along with physical, emotional, and sexual abuse were clarified. Prevalence rates among military populations were highlighted and include reported incidents of spousal, intimate partner, and adult sexual abuse. The context of violence and the numerous factors associated with military service were discussed along with its impact on victims' mental and physical health. Many of these factors also contribute to increased prevalence rates in areas including spouse abuse, intimate partner abuse, adult sexual abuse, and domestic abuse fatalities. The clinical implications, limitations, and future directions of DV and IVP will be illuminated in the last chapter of the brief.

Table 4.2 CDC risk and protective factors for intimate partner violence perpetration

Factors		List
Risk	Individual	Low self-esteem Low education or income Young age Aggressive or delinquent behavior as a youth Heavy alcohol and drug use Depression and suicide attempts Anger and hostility Lack of nonviolent social problem-solving skills Antisocial personality traits and conduct problems Poor behavioral control and impulsiveness Traits associated with borderline personality disorder History of being physically abusive Having few friends and being isolated from other people Economic stress (e.g., unemployment) Emotional dependence and insecurity Belief in strict gender roles (e.g., male dominance and aggression in relationships) Desire for power and control in relationships Hostility toward women Attitudes accepting or justifying violence and aggression History of physical or emotional abuse in childhood
	Relationship	Relationship conflicts including jealousy, possessiveness, tension, divorce, or separations Dominance and control of the relationship by one partner over the other Families experiencing economic stress Unhealthy family relationships and interactions Association with antisocial and aggressive peers Parents with less than a high school education Witnessing violence between parents as a child History of experiencing poor parenting as a child History of experiencing physical discipline as a child
	Community	Communities with high rates of poverty and limited educational and economic opportunities Communities with high unemployment rates Communities with high rates of violence and crime Communities where neighbors don't know or look out for each other and there is low community involvement among residents Communities with easy access to drugs and alcohol Weak community sanctions against IPV (e.g., unwillingness of neighbors to intervene in situations where they witness violence)
	Societal	Traditional gender norms and gender inequality (e.g., the idea women should stay at home, not enter the workforce, and be submissive; men should support the family and make the decisions) Cultural norms that support aggression toward others Societal income inequality Weak health, educational, economic, and social policies, or laws
Protective	Relationship	Strong social support networks and stable, positive relationships with other

(continued)

Table 4.2 (continued)

Factors		List
	Community	Neighborhood collective efficacy, meaning residents feel connected to each other and are involved in the community Coordination of resources and services among community agencies Communities with access to safe, stable housing Communities with access to medical care and mental health services Communities with access to economic and financial help

Note. Reprinted from Centers for Disease Control and Prevention (2021b)

References

Alhusen, J. L., Ray, E., Sharps, P., & Bullock, L. (2015). Intimate partner violence during pregnancy: Maternal and neonatal outcomes. *Journal of Women's Health, 24*(1), 100–106. https://doi.org/10.1089/jwh.2014.4872

Becker, P., & Bachman, R. (2019). Intimate partner violence in the military: An investigation of reporting crimes to law enforcement officials. *Journal of Family Violence, 35*(4), 315–324. https://doi.org/10.1007/s10896-019-00091-x

Burke, J., & Miller, A. R. (2016). *The effects of military change of station moves on spousal earnings*. RAND National Defense Research Institute Santa Monica United States. https://doi.org/10.7249/rb9920

Caetano, R., Schafer, J., Field, C., & Nelson, S. M. (2002). Agreement on reports of intimate partner violence among white, black, and Hispanic couples in the United States. *Journal of Interpersonal Violence, 17*(12), 1308–1322. https://doi.org/10.1177/088626002237858

Campbell, J. C., Garza, M. A., Gielen, A. C., O'Campo, P., Kub, J., Dienemann, J., Jones, A. S., & Jafar, E. (2003). Intimate partner violence and abuse among active-duty military women. *Violence Against Women, 9*(9), 1072–1092. https://doi.org/10.1177/1077801203255291

Centers for Disease Control and Prevention. (2021a, November 2). *Preventing intimate partner violence*. Centers for Disease Control and Prevention. Retrieved March 10, 2022, from https://www.cdc.gov/violenceprevention/intimatepartnerviolence/fastfact.html

Centers for Disease Control and Prevention. (2021b, November 2). *Risk and protective factors*. Centers for Disease Control and Prevention. Retrieved April 21, 2022, from https://www.cdc.gov/violenceprevention/intimatepartnerviolence/riskprotectivefactors.html

Chan, K. L. (2011). Gender differences in self-reports of intimate partner violence: A review. *Aggression and Violent Behavior, 16*(2), 167–175. https://doi.org/10.1016/j.avb.2011.02.008

Collette, T., Esenwein, S., Sprague-Jones, J., Moore, K., & Sterling, E. (2022). Incidence rates of emotional, sexual, and physical abuse in active-duty military service members, 1997–2015. *Aggression and Violent Behavior, 66*. https://doi.org/10.1016/j.avb.2022.101745

Cook, S. L., & Goodman, L. A. (2006). Beyond frequency and severity. *Violence Against Women, 12*(11), 1050–1072. https://doi.org/10.1177/1077801206293333

D'Inverno, A.S., Smith, S. G., and Zhang, X., (2019) *The impact of intimate partner violence: 2015 NSVS research-in-brief*. Centers for Disease Control and Prevention (CDC). https://www.cdc.gov/violenceprevention/pdf/nisvs/nisvs-impactbrief-508.pdf

Department of Defense. (2021). *Report on child abuse and neglect and domestic abuse in the military for fiscal year 2020*. https://download.militaryonesource.mil/12038/MOS/Reports/FINAL-DoD-FAP-Report-FY2020.pdf

Department of Defense Instruction (DoDI) 6400.03. (2014, April 25). *Family Advocacy Command Assistance Team* (*FACAT*), as amended.

Dichter, M. E., Cerulli, C., & Bossarte, R. M. (2011). Intimate partner violence victimization among women veterans and associated heart health risks. *Women's Health Issues, 21*(4). https://doi.org/10.1016/j.whi.2011.04.008

Dichter, M. E., Wagner, C., Borrero, S., Broyles, L., & Montgomery, A. E. (2017). Intimate partner violence, unhealthy alcohol use, and housing instability among women veterans in the veterans health administration. *Psychological Services, 14*(2), 246–249. https://doi.org/10.1037/ser0000132

DoDM 6400.01. (2016, August 11). Volume 3, "Family Advocacy Program (FAP): Clinical Case Staff Meeting (CCSM) and Incident Determination Committee (IDC)".

Dutton, M. A., & Goodman, L. A. (2005). Coercion in intimate partner violence: Toward a new conceptualization. *Sex Roles, 52*(11-12), 743–756. https://doi.org/10.1007/s11199-005-4196-6

Emery, C. R. (2009). Examining an extension of Johnson's hypothesis: Is male perpetrated intimate partner violence more underreported than female violence? *Journal of Family Violence, 25*(2), 173–181. https://doi.org/10.1007/s10896-009-9281-0

Fear, N. T., Iversen, A., Meltzer, H., Workman, L., Hull, L., Greenberg, N., Barker, C., Browne, T., Earnshaw, M., Horn, O., Jones, M., Murphy, D., Rona, R. J., Hotopf, M., & Wessely, S. (2007). Patterns of drinking in the UK armed forces. *Addiction, 102*(11), 1749–1759. https://doi.org/10.1111/j.1360-0443.2007.01978.x

Gerber, M. R., Iverson, K. M., Dichter, M. E., Klap, R., & Latta, R. E. (2014). Women veterans and intimate partner violence: Current state of knowledge and future directions. *Journal of Women's Health, 23*(4), 302–309. https://doi.org/10.1089/jwh.2013.4513

Gerlock, A. A. (2004). Domestic violence and post-traumatic stress disorder severity for participants of a domestic violence rehabilitation program. *Military Medicine, 169*(6), 470–474. https://doi.org/10.7205/milmed.169.6.470

Gierisch, J., Coeytaux, R., Urrutia, R., Havrilesky, L., Moorman, P., Lowery, W., Dinan, M., McBroom, A., Hasselblad, V., Sanders, G., & Myers, E. (2013). Oral contraceptive use and risk of breast, cervical, colorectal, and endometrial cancers: a systematic review. *Cancer Epidemiology Biomarkers Prevention, 22*(11), 1931–1943. https://doi.org/10.1158/1055-9965.EPI-13-0298. Epub 2013 Sep 6.

Hamrick, L. A., & Owens, G. P. (2019). Exploring the mediating role of selfblame and coping in the relationships between self-compassion and distress in females following the sexual assault. *Journal of Clinical Psychology, 75*(4), https://doi.org/10.1002/jclp.22730. Epub 2018 Dec 15

Hardesty, J. L., Crossman, K. A., Haselschwerdt, M. L., Raffaelli, M., Ogolsky, B. G., & Johnson, M. P. (2015). Toward a standard approach to operationalizing coercive control and classifying violence types. *Journal of Marriage and Family, 77*(4), 833–843. https://doi.org/10.1111/jomf.12201

Johnson, M. P. (2010). *Typology of domestic violence intimate terrorism, violent resistance, and situational couple violence*. Northeastern University Press.

Johnson, M. P. (2017). A personal social history of a typology of intimate partner violence. *Journal of Family Theory & Review, 9*(2), 150–164. https://doi.org/10.1111/jftr.12187

Johnson, M. P., & Leone, J. M. (2005). The differential effects of intimate terrorism and situational couple violence. *Journal of Family Issues, 26*(3), 322–349. https://doi.org/10.1177/0192513x04270345

Johnson, S. J., Sherman, M. D., Hoffman, J. S., James, L. C., Johnson, P. L., Lochman, J. E., et al. (2007). *The psychological needs of US military service members and their families: A preliminary report*. American Psychological Association. https://www.apa.org/about/policy/military-deployment-services.pdf

Jones, A. D. (2012). Intimate partner violence in military couples: A review of the literature. *Aggression and Violent Behavior, 17*(2), 147–157. https://doi.org/10.1016/j.avb.2011.12.002

Judkins, J., Smith, K., Moore, B. A., & Morissette, S. B. (2021). Alcohol use disorder in active duty service members: Incidence rates over a 19-year period. *Substance Abuse, 1–7*. https://doi.org/10.1080/08897077.2021.1941512

Kamarack, K.N., Ott, A., & Sacco, L.N., (2019). *Military families and intimate partner violence: Background and issues for congress*. (CRS Report No. R46097). Congressional Research Service. https://sgp.fas.org/crs/natsec/R46097.pdf

Kimerling, R., Iverson, K. M., Dichter, M. E., Rodriguez, A. L., Wong, A., & Pavao, J. (2016). Prevalence of intimate partner violence among women veterans who utilize veterans health administration primary care. *Journal of General Internal Medicine, 31*(8), 888–894. https://doi.org/10.1007/s11606-016-3701-7

Kwan, J., Sparrow, K., Facer-Irwin, E., Thandi, G., Fear, N. T., & MacManus, D. (2020). Prevalence of intimate partner violence perpetration among military populations: A systematic review and meta-analysis. *Aggression and Violent Behavior, 53*, 101419. https://doi.org/10.1016/j.avb.2020.101419

Lane, R., Short, R., Jones, M., Hull, L., Howard, L., Fear, N., & MacManus, D. (2022). Relationship conflict and partner violence by UK military personnel following return from deployment in Iraq and Afghanistan. *Social Psychiatry and Psychiatric Epidemiology, 57*, 1795–1805. https://doi.org/10.1016/j.avb.2020.101419

MacManus, D., Dean, K., Jones, M., Rona, R. J., Greenberg, N., Hull, L., Fahy, T., Wessely, S., & Fear, N. T. (2013). Violent offending by UK military personnel deployed to Iraq and Afghanistan: A data linkage cohort study. *The Lancet, 381*(9870), 907–917. https://doi.org/10.1016/s0140-6736(13)60354-2

Marshall, A., Panuzio, J., & Taft, C. (2005). Intimate partner violence among military veterans and active-duty servicemen. *Clinical Psychology Review, 25*(7), 862–876. https://doi.org/10.1016/j.cpr.2005.05.009

Office of the Secretary of Defense. (2021, December 15). *Domestic abuse involving Dod military and certain affiliated personnel*. (DoDI 6400.06). Department of Defense. https://www.esd.whs.mil/Portals/54/Documents/DD/issuances/dodi/640006p.pdf?ver=fy-sKxz8Z9ff-b_4fV6yHA%3d%3d

Okuda, M., Olfson, M., Wang, S., Rubio, J. M., Xu, Y., & Blanco, C. (2015). Correlates of intimate partner violence perpetration: Results from a national epidemiologic survey. *Journal of Traumatic Stress, 28*(1), 49–56. https://doi.org/10.1002/jts.21986

O'Leary, K. D., Tintle, N., & Bromet, E. (2014). Risk factors for physical violence against partners in the U.S. *Psychology of Violence, 4*(1), 65–77. https://doi.org/10.1037/a0034537

Orcutt, H. K., King, L. A., & King, D. W. (2003). Male-perpetrated violence among Vietnam veteran couples: Relationships with veteran's early life characteristics, trauma history, and PTSD symptomatology. *Journal of Traumatic Stress, 16*(4), 381–390. https://doi.org/10.1023/a:1024470103325

Parr, N. J., Young, S., Ward, R., & Mackey, K. (2021). *Evidence brief: Prevalence of intimate partner violence/sexual assault among veterans*. https://www.ncbi.nlm.nih.gov/books/NBK576986/

Pollard, R., & Ferguson, C. (2020). Intimate partner violence within Australian Defence Force families: An exploratory study. *Journal of Gender-Based Violence, 4*(2), 191–205. https://doi.org/10.1332/239868020X15850130841880

Sacco, L. N. (2015). *The violence against women act: Overview, legislation, and federal funding*. Congressional Research Service. https://www.utsystem.edu/sites/default/files/offices/police/files/annual-promotional-exams/vawa.pdf

Sayers, S. L., Farrow, V. A., Ross, J., & Oslin, D. W. (2009). Family problems among recently returned military veterans referred for a mental health evaluation. *The Journal of Clinical Psychiatry, 70*(2), 163–170. https://doi.org/10.4088/jcp.07m03863

Sexual assault in the military: Prevention: Hearing before the Military Personnel Subcommittee of the Committee on Armed Services, House of Representatives, 111th Cong. (Serial No. 111-17). (2009a). Retrieved from GPO's federal digital system: https://www.gpo.gov/fdsys/pkg/CHRG111hhrg52186/pdf/CHRG111hhrg52186.pdf

Sexual assault in the military: Victim support and advocacy: Hearing before the Military Personnel Subcommittee of the Committee on Armed Services, House of Representatives, 111th Cong. (Serial No. 111-4). (2009b). Retrieved from GPO's Federal Digital System: https://www.gpo.gov/fdsys/pkg/CHRG-111hhrg49634/pdf/CHRG111hhrg49634.pdf

Skomorovsky, A., Hujaleh, F., & Wolejszo, S. (2015). Intimate partner violence in the Canadian Armed Forces: The role of family stress and its impact on well-being. *Military Medicine, 180*(7), 809–816. https://doi.org/10.7205/MILMED-D-14-00447

Smith, S. G., Zhang, X., Basile, K. C., Merrick, M. T., Wang, J., Kresnow, M., & Chen, J. (2018). *The national intimate partner and sexual violence survey (NISVS): 2015 data brief – Updated release*. National Center for Injury Prevention and Control, Centers for Disease Control and Prevention. Retrieved from: https://www.cdc.gov/violenceprevention/pdf/2015data-brief508.pdf

Stark, E. (2009). *Coercive control: How men entrap women in personal life*. Oxford University Press.

Taft, C. T., Watkins, L. E., Stafford, J., Street, A. E., & Monson, C. M. (2011). Posttraumatic stress disorder and intimate relationship problems: A meta-analysis. *Journal of Consulting and Clinical Psychology, 79*(1), 22–33. https://doi.org/10.1037/a0022196

Tinney, G., & Gerlock, A. A. (2014). Intimate partner violence, military personnel, veterans, and their families. *Family Court Review, 52*(3), 400–416.

Tong, P., Payne, L., Bond, C., Meadows, S., Lewis, J., Friedman, E., & Maksabedian Hernandez, E. (2018). *Enhancing family stability during a permanent change of station: A review of disruptions and policies*. https://doi.org/10.7249/rr2304.

Whitaker, M. P. (2013). Motivational attributions about intimate partner violence among male and female perpetrators. *Journal of Interpersonal Violence, 29*(3), 517–535. https://doi.org/10.1177/0886260513505211

Wright, K. M., Foran, H. M., Wood, M. D., Eckford, R. D., & McGurk, D. (2012). Alcohol problems, aggression, and other externalizing behaviors after return from deployment: Understanding the role of combat exposure, internalizing symptoms, and social environment. *Journal of Clinical Psychology, 68*(7), 782–800. https://doi.org/10.1002/jclp.21864

Chapter 5
Violent Criminal Behavior in the Military

Violence in the military is a prevalent occurrence, often leading to involvement with the criminal justice system or significant psychosocial consequences for this population. According to 2016 statistics from the Bureau of Justice, there were over 100,000 veterans incarcerated in the United States (Maruschak et al., 2021). In general, veterans who are at an increased risk of criminal offending and incarceration are more often male, single, have a lower level of education, and experience symptoms of mental illness (Greenberg & Rosenheck, 2009; Lucas et al., 2022). The average age of male veterans incarcerated in 2016 was 51 years old in federal and 52 years old in state prisons, both more than a decade older than nonveteran offenders (Maruschak et al., 2021). However, current research on age as a risk factor for criminal offending and incarceration of veterans is mixed (Lucas et al., 2022). For example, one study indicated that veterans who demonstrated greater criminal justice involvement were younger (Greenberg & Rosenheck, 2009), while other studies established that incarcerated veterans are typically 10–12 years older than nonveteran inmates (Lucas et al., 2022; Noonan & Mumola, 2007; White et al., 2012).

Findings on the race of incarcerated veterans are also inconsistent throughout the literature (Lucas et al., 2022). In 2016, 50% of male veterans serving time in state or federal prison were White. In addition, approximately 23% of incarcerated veterans were Black, and 10% in state and 12% in federal prisons were Hispanic (Maruschak et al., 2021). Furthermore, fewer than 3% of male veterans incarcerated in these facilities in 2016 identified as American Indian or Alaskan Native, and about 1% identified as Asian, Hawaiian Native, or Pacific Islander. Of note, approximately 14% of male veterans in state prison and 12% in federal prison in 2016 identified as two or more races. While these figures align with results across studies (Greenberg & Rosenheck, 2009; Lucas et al., 2022; Noonan & Mumola, 2007; White et al., 2012), Greenberg and Rosenheck (2009) highlight the increased risk of criminal justice involvement that veterans of minority racial groups face by comparing groups of incarcerated and non-incarcerated groups of veterans.

M. T. Baker et al., *Violence in the Military*, SpringerBriefs in Psychology,
https://doi.org/10.1007/978-3-031-26883-0_5

In 2019, 10,252 veterans were federal offenders in the Federal Bureau of Prisons (BOP), with over 4% serving sentences for a felony or Class A misdemeanor (Schmitt & Kerbel, 2021). These individuals were separated from the military for an average of 23 years before committing the federal offense (Schmitt & Kerbel, 2021). According to the Bureau of Justice statistics, over half of incarcerated veterans served in the Army, and between 20% and 30% were combat veterans (Maruschak et al., 2021). Honorable discharge was the most common discharge type among male veterans serving time in state and federal prisoners (Maruschak et al., 2021). Interestingly, the types of crimes committed by incarcerated veterans appear to be distinct from their civilian counterparts.

The Bureau of Justice statistics from 2016 indicate that about 70% of all male state prisoners were serving sentences for violent offenses, compared to 56.7% of nonveteran inmates (Maruschak et al., 2021). Of male federal prisoners, veterans were more than twice as likely to commit a violent offense, compared to their nonveteran counterparts (Maruschak et al., 2021). Furthermore, over 7% of male veteran federal prisoners committed violent sexual offenses, compared to about 1% of male nonveteran federal prisoners (Maruschak et al., 2021). Between the years 2005 and 2007, there were 121 homicides committed by Iraq and Afghanistan war veterans (Sreenivasan et al., 2013). Of these homicide cases, over half (56%) were first-degree murder charges, and 21% were charges of manslaughter due to the perpetrator driving while intoxicated (Sreenivasan et al., 2013).

Of all veterans incarcerated in federal prison in 2019, 11.6% committed crimes related to child pornography (Schmitt & Kerbel, 2021). These veterans were four times more likely than nonveteran prisoners to commit crimes of child pornography and twice as likely to commit sexual abuse offenses (Schmitt & Kerbel, 2021). In addition, about 43% of male veterans in state prisons, and 17% in federal prisons, were serving sentences for violent crimes other than sexual offenses (Maruschak et al., 2021).

In 2016, about 30% of veterans incarcerated in federal prisons were serving sentences for a drug offense (Maruschak et al., 2021). Drug trafficking was identified as the most common crime type for veterans in federal courts who committed a felony or Class A misdemeanor in 2019 (Schmitt & Kerbel, 2021). In addition, over 8% of male veterans incarcerated in state prisons were serving sentences for drug-related offenses (Maruschak et al., 2021).

As of 2016, statistics indicate that veteran federal prisoners were twice as likely to commit a property offense compared to male nonveterans (Maruschak et al., 2021). Specifically, over 9% of male veterans in state prisons, and over 12% in federal prisons, were serving sentences for a property offense (Maruschak et al., 2021). About 18% of veterans incarcerated in federal prisons for a felony or Class A misdemeanor charge were sentenced for fraud (Schmitt & Kerbel, 2021). Of the same group, almost 14% of veterans were sentenced for charges related to firearms.

A 2010 report from the Defence Analytical Services and Advice (DASA) that examined ex-Armed Forces prisoners who were subject to probation in England and Wales found similar types of crime being committed by soldiers. The report indicated that 3.5% of prisoners in these countries were former soldiers of the United

Kingdom (UK) Regular Armed Forces (DASA, 2010). The offense group that was committed at the highest rate (18.8%) among the veteran prisoners was violence against another person, which includes crimes ranging from assault to murder (DASA, 2010). Of note, sexual offenses were committed by 5.1% of the veteran prisoners and represented the fourth largest offense group among the sample (DASA, 2010).

Relevantly, prior research on violence in military members has explored potentially criminal behavior, despite any known involvement in the criminal justice system. For example, Taft et al. (2007) conducted a study on overt aggressive behavior in a sample of 1168 treatment-seeking veterans. The participants were actively engaged in VA services including psychiatry, posttraumatic stress treatment, substance abuse treatment, or counseling. Over 65% of participants endorsed being verbally abusive in the past 6 months (Taft et al., 2007). Several other seriously aggressive acts were also reported, such as threatening someone with physical violence (42.2%), destroying property (23.4%), physically fighting with someone (24.3%), and threatening or using a weapon against someone (11.5–4.4%; Taft et al., 2007). Although researchers did not explore prior criminal history or possible repercussions of these behaviors, these reported aggressive acts are consistent with the data on the types of criminal offenses veterans commit.

High-profile violent offenses committed by military personnel have triggered a more forceful investigation into the factors impacting the rates of violence and aggression among this population (MacManus et al., 2015). For example, between the years 2006 and 2009, nine US service members of Fort Carson committed or were charged with murder after returning from Iraq (Alvarez & Frosch, 2009). In 2009, soldiers from the 5th Stryker Brigade at Fort Lewis conspired to create a "kill team" and murder civilians (ref.), ultimately ending in incarceration (Boal, 2011). An increase in serious violent crimes, including domestic violence, rape, and sexual assault was also observed. These incidents sparked consideration for the need to review the history of all Army personnel who committed violent offenses after returning from Iraq or Afghanistan to gain a better understanding of the factors underlying the perpetration of violence (Alvarez & Frosch, 2009). These circumstances are not unique to the US military, as in 2012, while on leave after being involved in a bombing that killed six servicemen in Afghanistan, a soldier of the British Army was arrested after he was suspected of stabbing his girlfriend to death, inflicting ten injuries (GMT, 2012). The soldier was subsequently convicted and sentenced to 28 years (GMT, 2012). The popular media coverage elicited by this event and concerns from the public and political figures contributed to a push for understanding the impact deployment and combat exposure has on soldiers' mental health and risk for violence (MacManus et al., 2015).

Other types of offenses, although occurring less frequently, raise a substantial concern about violence among military personnel. An example of domestic terrorism and gun violence in the military was demonstrated on November 5, 2009, in Fort Hood, Texas, after a commissioned officer in the US Army opened fire on unarmed military members and civilians. The shooting resulted in 13 casualties and 42 wounded individuals. The importance of anticipating acts of violence by military members became even more urgent following this event. Despite this, aggression and violence continue with the recent death of Vanessa Guillen at Fort Hood.

In 2010, the Department of Defense (DoD) published an independent review related to the events at Fort Hood. This review recommended the development of interventions for violence risk reduction in military populations (DoD, 2010; Elbogen et al., 2012a). Furthermore, this review highlighted indicators for violence and briefly discussed theories relating to a person's motivation to engage in violence (DoD, 2010). Importantly, the review made note that it is often the combination of different risk factors that leads to violence. Specifically, the review named the following as established reasons why people commit violence: genetic and biological causes; mental illness and personality disorders; substance use; religious, social, and political motivations; and environmental factors (DoD, 2010).

The events at Fort Hood, the killing leading to the arrest of a British Army serviceman, and the murders linked to the soldiers of Fort Carson and Fort Lewis are examples that create an urgency to understand and mitigate the commission of violence among military members. In addition, the prevalence of incarcerated military personnel in the United States also delivers a strong rationale for addressing this topic. To date, researchers have attempted to identify variables that put military members at risk of post-service criminal offending to begin delineating the issue of violence among this population.

5.1 Risk Factors for Violent Crime

The literature that discusses risk factors for criminal behavior and incarceration of military members is expansive. According to Coté et al. (2020), criminogenic risk factors for the incarceration of veterans include prior criminal history, mental health problems, homelessness, and drug and alcohol abuse. Similarly, Lucas et al. (2022) named mental illness and substance abuse as significant predictors of criminal justice involvement in veteran populations. One study identified exposure to military sexual trauma (MST), PTSD, traumatic brain injury (TBI), and clinically significant levels of pain as strongly related to legal problems (Backhaus et al., 2016). In a sample of homeless veterans with a criminal history, psychiatric hospitalizations and substance use were significant predictors of criminal offending, with a history of mental illness exacerbating the risk of criminal justice involvement (Benda et al., 2003). Another study found that veterans with PTSD and negative affect were more likely to be arrested and identified drug use and criminal history as strong predictors of arrest (Elbogen et al., 2012b). According to Erickson et al. (2008), substance abuse and major depression were independently and significantly associated with incarceration in a sample of veterans being treated at an inpatient VA hospital. Meanwhile, Black et al. (2005) identified psychiatric and medical comorbidity as an important factor related to incarceration rates in a sample of veterans. Overall, mental health and substance use problems have been frequently associated with an increased risk of incarceration among military populations.

Other risk factors for violent and aggressive behaviors by military members have been identified. For example, in a study examining US veterans' risk for severe and physical violence, younger age, prior criminal history, combat exposure, posttraumatic stress symptomatology, alcohol abuse, and homelessness were all associated with increased risk (Elbogen et al., 2012a). Smith et al. (2021) suggested that new soldiers who displayed episodes of anger attacks are often younger, male, non-Hispanic White, of lower educational attainment, and unmarried, compared to those who have not experienced anger attacks. Compared to civilians, factors that contribute to violence in military populations are unique. For example, military members experience service-related factors, such as deployment and combat exposure, that may aid in the development of violent behavior through increased exposure to trauma and stress. Military members also face significant stressors and barriers at discharge and post-service that may also contribute to future violence.

5.2 Factors Contributing to Violence

5.2.1 Aggression

As discussed, incarcerated veterans are more likely than nonveterans to serve sentences for a violent offense (Maruschak et al., 2021). In addition, there have been significant incidents related to military violent behavior, such as the shootings at Fort Hood in 2009, that warrant further investigation of aggression concerning violence in the military (Elbogen et al., 2012a). Aggression has been defined in social psychology as "any behavior directed towards another individual carried out with immediate intent to cause harm" whereby "the perpetrator must believe that the behavior will harm the target and that the target is motivated to avoid the behavior" (Anderson & Bushman, 2002, pp. 357–358).

Current literature has begun to demonstrate how aggression and violence are often seen in military populations (Elbogen et al., 2012a; Gallaway et al., 2012; MacManus et al., 2015; Thomas et al., 2010). For example, in a sample of 1388 military veterans, 33% reported that they committed a recent act of non-combat-related violence or aggression, while 11% of the sample reportedly engaged in severe violent acts (Elbogen et al., 2012a). Similarly, in a study of overt aggression in US Army soldiers, participants most frequently reported aggressive acts of grabbing someone or throwing something at someone (Gallaway et al., 2012). According to Thomas et al. (2010), soldiers returning home from deployment appeared to demonstrate a high frequency of aggressive behavior. Specifically, 43% of the sample endorsed being physically violent with objects as a result of becoming angry with someone (Thomas et al., 2010). In addition, 38% of participants reportedly made threats of physical violence to another, while 18% of soldiers indicated that they engaged in physical violence by hitting another person during a fight.

Another study examined the frequency of "anger attacks" demonstrated by a large sample of new soldiers (Smith et al., 2021). Individuals were identified as having displayed anger attacks if they had difficulty controlling their anger, became angry in a situation where most people would not, or experienced a high number of outbursts. Results indicated that soldiers who endorsed anger attacks were more likely to display "impairing" episodes, which were defined as outbursts that interfered with their work or personal life (Smith et al., 2021). Furthermore, in the same sample, approximately one-quarter of the soldiers with a history of anger endorsed experiencing more than 50 attacks throughout their life (Smith et al., 2021). Finally, a systematic review from 2015 highlights the prevalence of aggression and violent behavior among both the US and UK military populations (MacManus et al., 2015). According to the researchers, studies consistently found that aggression and violent behavior is prevalent among both active-duty soldiers and veterans (MacManus et al., 2015). Although definitions and measures of violence and aggression vary throughout the literature, current research highlights the frequency of these behaviors, which warrants further investigation and intervention of these behaviors (MacManus et al., 2015).

The evidence supporting aggression as a significant risk factor for violence in military populations is substantial, and the two often coincide. As such, the following discussion will explore risk factors for violence, as well as aggressive behavior, among this population. The subsequent sections will address how service-related factors, such as pre-enlistment history, deployment and combat exposure, discharge deposition, and mental illness, have been recognized as contributing to military members' risk for violence.

5.2.2 Service-Related Factors

Prior research on violence in the military discusses the extent to which service-related factors, such as pre-enlistment history, deployment and combat exposure, and discharge deposition, contribute to this phenomenon. Understanding how these factors correlate with aggression and contribute to violence can provide essential information for creating prevention and intervention strategies to help mitigate future risks in this population.

5.2.2.1 Pre-enlistment History

Before enlisting, some soldiers display behaviors and attitudes or experience life events that may put them at a greater risk for engaging in violence during service or post-discharge. For example, the current literature indicates that a history of aggressive or violent behavior before military enlistment is associated with these behaviors later in life (MacManus et al., 2012; Smith et al., 2021). Additionally, soldiers who exhibit difficulty controlling anger, inappropriate expression of anger, or high frequency of angry outbursts, before enlistment, are at an increased risk for suicidality (Smith et al., 2021).

Pre-enlistment behaviors and attitudes related to antisocial personality disorder, such as delinquency, aggressiveness, and a disregard for the safety of others, may be especially influential in military members' risk for violence (APA, 2013; MacManus et al., 2012). In a sample of active-duty and reservists from the United Kingdom, researchers found that about 18% demonstrated "pre-enlistment antisocial behaviors," which consisted of getting into fights and leaving school without explanation, being expelled or suspended, or engaging in behaviors that should have or warranted police involvement (MacManus et al., 2012, p. 1355). According to the study, soldiers who displayed pre-enlistment antisocial behaviors were about twice as likely to report severe alcohol use, risky driving, angry outbursts, and a history of assault that led to hospitalization, than those who did not display such behaviors before enlisting (MacManus et al., 2012). MacManus and colleagues concluded that individuals who displayed antisocial behavior, including aggression and violence, before joining the military, were more likely to continue demonstrating those behaviors later in life. Interestingly, they also found that pre-enlistment antisocial behaviors were associated with being more likely to discharge a weapon during combat (MacManus et al., 2012). Results from this research suggest that antisocial traits or tendencies may be a risk factor for violence in the military, especially if the individual exhibits a history of these attitudes and behaviors (see Personality Disorders subsection).

It is worth noting that service members who exhibit pre-enlistment antisocial behaviors are likely to have been displaying similar tendencies throughout childhood and adolescence, given the typical age at enlistment. Among civilian populations, it has been established that disruptive and conduct disorders displayed during childhood are often associated with an increased likelihood of antisocial and criminal behavior in adulthood (Reef et al., 2011; Simonoff et al., 2004). Some research has attributed the development of antisocial and behavioral problems to adverse experiences during childhood. As such, it is important to consider the impact of negative childhood experiences while discussing risk factors for violence among military populations.

Research highlights the effect adversity during childhood and "polyvictimization" has on the manifestation of behavioral difficulties (Lovallo, 2013; Ross et al., 2018). Specifically, it is suggested that structural changes in the brain due to stress and trauma during childhood can contribute to emotion dysregulation, problems with self-control, and the development of antisocial tendencies (Lovallo, 2013). Indeed, a history of childhood abuse experienced by military personnel has been related to subsequent suicidality and violent impulses in a sample of US veterans (Elbogen et al., 2018b). In a study exploring the differential impact of childhood abuse on suicidality between Canadian Armed Forces personnel and the Canadian general population, results indicate childhood abuse exposure is higher among soldiers compared to the general population and that these adverse experiences are associated with increased rates of suicidality in both samples (Afifi et al., 2016). Relevantly, anger and hostility constructs are found to be significantly associated with being physically or sexually abused during childhood or adolescence, or with witnessing family violence (Elbogen et al., 2010).

The impact that early negative life events have on criminality, including violent charges, was explored in a sample of 20 discharged military personnel who were incarcerated (Wainwright et al., 2016). Of the 20 veterans, 13 committed violent offenses including violence against another person or a sexual offense. During interviews with the participants, adverse events in the home or at school were frequently reported. Factors such as experiencing the loss of a caretaker at a young age, physical or sexual abuse during childhood, or being bullied at school were endorsed by some participants (Wainwright et al., 2016). The researchers referenced the impact these events may have had on the veterans' vulnerability for criminal behavior, as pre-service trauma and adversity emerged as a consistent theme across interviews.

As indicated, it is likely that pre-enlistment behaviors or traits, such as antisocial tendencies, and early negative life events, have a significant impact on the risk for violence among military members. Understanding these pre-enlistment factors helps elucidate those that can be assessed before enlisting in the military and monitored during service to help mitigate potential violence. In addition, intervention strategies provided to new soldiers who present with these qualities upon enlistment may help reduce their overall risk of engaging in future violent behavior.

5.2.2.2 Deployment and Combat Exposure

Deployment and combat exposure are factors frequently explored concerning the risk of violence among military populations. A common rationale for the assumed relationship between combat exposure and violence among military members is a service member's mindset and the habituation to aggressive and violent behaviors (Currier et al., 2014; Sreenivasan et al., 2013; Wainwright et al., 2016). Often referred to as "battle-mind," service members are taught survival skills to help build their resiliency while facing danger and adversity during combat. In addition, service members with combat exposure have repeatedly learned to engage in adaptive coping mechanisms elicited by the body's natural reaction to a perceived threat. Military personnel often experience heightened adrenaline states and hypervigilance during these times, which helps them react quickly, often with lethal means, to better protect themselves and fellow service members (Sreenivasan et al., 2013). Although essential in a combat zone, these behaviors can be maladaptive in civilian settings and may lead to prolonged states of paranoia and stress, aggressive behaviors, and lethal means of violence (Sreenivasan et al., 2013). Indeed, enhancing self-regulatory processes (i.e., up- and downregulation) has become a pillar of current health-oriented programs like the Master Resilience Training and Holistic Health and Fitness (H2F) programs.

Overall, the literature presents complex results in terms of deployment and combat exposure as contributing factors for violence among military personnel. One study found a significant relationship between engagement in violent combat and verbal aggression of soldiers (Killgore et al., 2008). However, this type of combat exposure was not significantly related to more physical acts of aggression, such as kicking or smashing objects, hitting someone, or threats of physical violence (Killgore et al., 2008). Another study demonstrated how soldiers who experienced the "highest levels of combat intensity" reported higher frequency of minor and severe overt acts of physical aggression (p. 362) (Killgore et al., 2008). In the same study, soldiers who did not deploy or who experienced a lower level of combat intensity reported relatively less physical aggression. Similarly, in a study aimed to examine the risk factors for violence among war veterans, results found that combat exposure is significantly related to engaging in non-combat severe violent acts, such as using a deadly weapon, threatening someone with a gun or knife, or physically injuring someone (Elbogen et al., 2012a). Although combat exposure was identified as a risk factor for violence, results from this study emphasized the importance of understanding the combination of both risk and protective factors for a more accurate depiction of a veteran's risk for violent behavior.

Due to the multifaceted nature of previous findings, the direct impact of deployment and combat exposure on the risk for violence and aggression in military service members is unclear. For example, Taft et al. (2007) debate that the association between more severe levels of combat exposure and committing aggressive acts is exclusively explained by the presence of higher posttraumatic stress symptoms, which can consist of a range of presentations. Whereas MacManus et al. (2012) argue that the increased risk for criminality and violence among service members may be more accurately attributed to underlying antisocial traits, rather than combat exposure. Research supporting this hypothesis has demonstrated that a history of antisocial behaviors and attitudes better explained the presence of these behaviors in the future than did combat exposure (Fontana & Rosenheck, 2005). These findings add complexity to understanding the causal relationship between combat experience, personality traits, psychopathology, and service members' risk for violence. Nevertheless, given the relevance of deployment and combat exposure within the context of military personnel, even indirect relationships between these factors and violence need to be thoroughly considered when discussing the risk.

5.2.2.3 Discharge Deposition

Discharge deposition has been less frequently explored as a contributing factor to violence among military populations. However, the potential impact that discharge status may have on service members' transition into civilian life is substantial. Service members are most frequently separated from the military under honorable conditions, with approximately 85% receiving an honorable discharge upon satisfying their service (Holliday & Pedersen, 2017). Despite the high frequency of service members being honorably discharged, a portion of service members is separated from the military under less than favorable conditions. Service members who obtain a *general*, *other than honorable*, or *dishonorable* discharge may face consequences ranging from ineligibility for certain veteran benefits to significant psychosocial stressors upon separation from the military (Brooks Holliday & Pedersen, 2017).

Veterans with a discharge status of dishonorable were likely to have violated the Uniform Code of Military Justice (UCMJ) and faced court-martial proceedings. Furthermore, bad conduct suggests the service member was discharged for significant disciplinary problems, which may include misconduct or criminal behavior (Brooks Holliday & Pedersen, 2017). A discharge status of other than honorable or dishonorable raises questions about the type of behavior the service members exhibited before discharge, which may have resulted in separation from the military.

Overall, studies indicate that service members who did not receive an honorable discharge experienced higher rates of mental health issues (Booth-Kewley et al., 2010; Brooks Holliday & Pedersen, 2017). In addition, discharges of bad conduct were predicted by mental health diagnosis and early combat experience (Booth-Kewley et al., 2010). As previously discussed, combat exposure, especially coupled with mental health difficulties, can contribute to the risk of future violence among military personnel. Furthermore, the literature suggests that psychiatric diagnoses may make service members more vulnerable to experiencing behavioral problems such as impulsivity, antisocial tendencies, and disruptive behaviors (Booth-Kewley et al., 2010). Discharge status was also previously associated with violence toward the self, in that a non-routine discharge was significantly predictive of not only psychiatric illness and substance use but also suicidality (Brignone et al., 2017).

Broadly, military personnel with psychiatric diagnoses are at greater risk for experiencing psychosocial difficulties, such as homelessness, substance abuse, and incarceration (Benda et al., 2003; Edwards et al., 2021; Elbogen et al., 2012b, 2018a). As such, a discharge status of other than honorable, dishonorable, or bad conduct are likely to contribute to substantial problems with adjustment to civilian life. Overall, service-related factors such as pre-enlistment history, deployment and combat experience, and discharge deposition are likely to contribute both directly and indirectly to violent behavior among military personnel. The following sections aim to further explore the aforementioned mental health disorders that have been attributed to violence in the military.

5.2.3 Mental Health

According to current literature, mental health disorders are among the top diagnoses that veterans obtain while receiving care from Veterans Affairs (VA) clinics (Brancu et al., 2017). In a large sample of veterans ($N = 103{,}788$) being treated at a VA between the years 2001 and 2005, 25% were diagnosed with one or more psychiatric disorders (Seal et al., 2007). PTSD (13%) was the most frequently diagnosed disorder in the sample, followed by anxiety (6%), adjustment disorder (6%), depression (5%), and substance use disorder (5%; Seal et al., 2007). Thirteen percent of the sample was identified as having psychosocial or behavioral problems that may warrant mental health treatment, although these veterans did not meet the criteria for a mental illness (Seal et al., 2007). In a more recent study of treatment-seeking, non-deployed, US military personnel, including both veterans and active-duty service members, diagnostic criteria were most frequently met for PTSD (26%), followed by major depressive disorder (MDD; 22%), anxiety (no PTSD; 11.8%), alcohol abuse and/or dependence (6%), adjustment disorder (2.1%), and cannabis abuse/dependence (1.5%; Brancu et al., 2017). Although beyond this scope of this brief, for recent data on behavioral health concerns and correlates in the active force as a whole, we refer readers to recently published epidemiologic data on PTSD (Judkins et al., 2020), postpartum depression (Nicholsonn et al., 2020), alcohol use (Judkins et al., 2020), chronic pain conditions (Moore et al., 2019), sleep disorders (Moore et al., 2021), and anxiety disorders (Russell et al., 2022). These figures provide concrete evidence for the prevalence of mental illness among active-duty service members and veterans. Although military personnel experience a range of mental health disorders, some psychiatric illnesses consist of diagnostic criteria specifically related to excessive anger and often manifest as problems with emotional or behavioral regulation.

Posttraumatic stress disorder (PTSD), TBI, antisocial personality disorder (ASPD), and substance use disorders have all been recognized by the *Diagnostic and Statistical Manual of Mental Disorders, Fifth Edition*, (*DSM-5*; American Psychological Association [APA], 2013) as possessing symptoms related to aggression or contributing to psychosocial forms of aggressive behavior. For example, according to the *DSM-5*, PTSD symptoms can consist of changes in arousal or reactivity. These symptoms may present as irritability, angry outbursts, recklessness, or self-destructive behavior (APA, 2013), all of which are behaviors that may contribute to violence against the self or others. Similarly, TBI is associated with an increased risk of emotional and behavioral problems, including irritability and aggression (APA, 2013). In addition, ASPD is characterized by behaviors that disregard or violate the rights of others (APA, 2013). Furthermore, individuals with ASPD often demonstrate irritability or aggressive behavior in the form of physical violence or assaults (APA, 2013). Finally, the *DSM-5* indicates that substance use disorders can also lead to social and interpersonal problems, such as engagement in violent arguments or abuse while intoxicated (APA, 2013). Relevantly, research on veterans with serious mental illness indicates that violence perpetrated by this population was related to PTSD, head injury, and substance use (Elbogen et al., 2008).

As previously discussed in this chapter, aggression and aggressive behaviors have been identified as factors contributing to violence in military members. Research has highlighted the association between some mental disorders and increased aggression or violence. Based on the prevalence rates of these disorders among military personnel, and the presence of diagnostic criteria related to aggression, it is noteworthy to investigate these mental illnesses as potential risk factors for violent behavior. The following sections will provide evidence for how mental disorders such as PTSD, TBI, personality disorders, and substance use are relevant risk factors contributing to violence in the military.

5.2.3.1 Posttraumatic Stress Disorder

A systematic literature review that examined data from 38 recent articles identified the 12-month prevalence of PTSD for military populations to range from 6.7% to 50.2%, compared to a range of 2.3% to 9.1% among civilian populations (Schein et al., 2021). More broadly, the *DSM-5* identifies the 12-month prevalence of PTSD for US adults to be about 3.5% (APA, 2013). Several studies throughout the literature have linked PTSD and associated symptoms to aggression in military populations (Castillo et al., 2002; Novaco & Chembtob, 2002; Orth & Wieland, 2006; Taft et al., 2007). An early study found that elevated scores on a multi-dimensional assessment of anger were related to the presence of PTSD symptomology in a group of Vietnam veterans (McFall et al., 1999a). A more recent meta-analysis from 2006 provided evidence of an apparent correlation between PTSD and anger and hostility in individuals with trauma exposure (Orth & Wieland, 2006). This relationship was consistent in another study, where male veterans with a diagnosis of PTSD scored higher on a measure of anger and hostility than those with other psychiatric disorders (Castillo et al., 2002). Similarly, in a sample of Iraq and Afghanistan War veterans, those who met PTSD criteria, and those who were "sub-threshold," endorsed significantly greater levels of anger and hostility than those without PTSD symptoms (Jakupcak et al., 2007). Interestingly, PTSD symptom severity has been significantly associated with anger, even after aggression-related items were removed from PTSD measures (Novaco & Chembtob, 2002). This suggests that the relationship between PTSD and anger is not solely related to overlapping in measurement used during the assessment.

Early research has already highlighted the relationship between PTSD and violence in military veterans (Beckham et al., 1997; McFall et al., 1999b). One study found that combat-exposed veterans with PTSD committed a significantly higher number of violent acts toward another person (e.g., throwing something at someone, pushing grabbing, shoving, slapping, kicking, biting, hitting, beating up, threatening with a gun or knife, using a gun or knife on someone) than those without PTSD (Beckham et al., 1997). Specifically, veterans with a PTSD diagnosis reported engaging in an average of 22 acts of interpersonal violence in the past year, while the control group without such a diagnosis reportedly committed less than 1 (Beckham et al., 1997). In a sample of 118 Vietnam veterans seeking outpatient treatment, more severe PTSD symptomology and higher levels of verbal aggression were significantly correlated with engagement in interpersonal violence (Beckham et al., 1997). Another study found that veterans seeking inpatient psychiatric treatment committed a higher number of violent acts (e.g., property destruction, threats with or without a weapon, physical assault) than inpatient veterans with other mental health disorders (McFall et al., 1999b). In addition, in a sample of anger treatment-seeking male veterans, those with PTSD scored higher than veterans with other mental health diagnoses on subscales of anger, including assault, which consisted of physical violation of another, and verbal hostility, such as arguing, cursing, threatening, and shouting (Castillo et al., 2002).

Currently, studies continue to find strong associations between posttraumatic stress and violent behavior in military populations (Bennett et al., 2018; Gallaway et al., 2012). For example, in a sample of 697 justice-involved veterans with either military or non-military-related trauma exposure, PTSD symptoms of intrusion, avoidance, and arousal were positively associated with violent offenses, but not nonviolent offenses (Bennett et al., 2018). Furthermore, Gallaway et al. (2012) found that active-duty service members who endorsed behavioral health issues, including posttraumatic stress, reported higher frequencies of minor and severe forms of physical aggression. Since physical aggression can easily manifest as violence toward another person, this study provides further evidence for the association between PTSD and violence among active-duty service members. In addition, several studies have identified a relationship between PTSD and veterans engaging in acts of intimate partner violence (MacManus et al., 2015; Sexton et al., 2019). Interestingly, results from one study found a significant positive relationship between having violent social networks (e.g., friends, family members, co-workers, neighbors, etc., who get into physical fights) and engaging in physical aggression toward a partner (Sexton et al., 2019). These results were observed if the veteran endorsed symptoms that indicated a probable PTSD diagnosis, but not if they screened negative for the disorder (Sexton et al., 2019). This indicates that it is possible veterans with a diagnosis of PTSD may be more susceptible to the influence of a violent social network and experience increased engagement in similar behaviors.

Interestingly, the various symptom clusters of PTSD (e.g., hyperarousal, intrusion, avoidance, and numbing) have been explored independently as risk factors for aggression and violence in military populations (Bennett et al., 2018; Taft et al., 2007). For example, hyperarousal symptoms, specifically anger and irritability, have been strongly related to general aggression in military populations (Taft et al., 2007, 2009). Research demonstrates the extent to which hyperarousal symptoms are significantly and positively related to aggression in a sample of veterans (Taft et al., 2007). In addition, an increase in intrusion symptom severity has been associated with marked increases in the likelihood of veterans being charged with a violent offense (Bennett et al., 2018). Research has also found that higher levels of avoidance or numbing symptoms are negatively associated with aggression (Taft et al., 2007). These results demonstrate the variability of symptom presentations among individuals diagnosed with PTSD. With a range of diagnostic criteria, individuals with PTSD are often observed displaying differences in symptomatology, as well as how they express those symptoms. Individuals who experience higher levels of avoidance or numbing symptoms may be more likely to exhibit internalized distress, rather than externalizing their suffering through behaviors such as violent acts (MacManus et al., 2015).

As demonstrated throughout this section, PTSD has consistently been attributed to violence among military personnel. The extensive amount of evidence highlights the considerable need for violence prevention and treatment strategies for service members and veterans who exhibit symptoms of posttraumatic stress.

5.2.3.2 Traumatic Brain Injury

Traumatic brain injury (TBI) is a type of neurocognitive disorder worthy of discussion when exploring factors likely to contribute to violence in the military. TBI is characterized by a head injury with accompanying loss of consciousness, posttraumatic amnesia, disorientation, and confusion, or other neurological symptoms (APA, 2013). Statistics from the US Department of Veterans Affairs indicate that approximately 414,000 TBIs have been endured by military personnel between the years 2000 and 2019 (US Department of Veterans Affairs, n.d.). In a study examining the prevalence rates of TBI among 188 US veterans, ages 51 and older, approximately 36% of the sample endorsed having a lifetime history of TBI, and about 71% reportedly experienced a head or neck injury at some point in their lives (Kornblith et al., 2020).

Generally, damage to the brain, specifically areas of the frontal and temporal lobes, has been understood to result in emotional dysfunction, including diminished anger control and anger outbursts (Iverson, 2010). In military populations, brain injury has been linked to a difficulty controlling anger, general aggression, and arrests in military personnel (Bailie et al., 2015; Elbogen et al., 2012b). Bailie et al. (2015) studied the impact of TBI on service members' experience of anger, including their patterns of expressing anger and their ability to control anger impulsivity. Results from the study indicate that service members with a history of TBI reported higher levels of state and trait anger when compared to service members without a history of head injury. Service members with a history of TBI also endorsed increased outward and internal expression of anger and lower inhibition of anger (Bailie et al., 2015). Relevant to self-directed violence, a recent study found that rates of suicide were more than double for veterans with a history of TBI, compared to those without such a history (Hostetter et al., 2019). Figures from the US Department of Veterans' Affairs estimated that veterans were up to 2.45 times more likely to die by suicide if they had a history of moderate to severe TBI than those without a TBI (US Department of Veterans Affairs, n.d.).

The psychological and behavioral sequelae of TBI is especially complicated for military personnel by way of frequent comorbid mental illness, such as PTSD, and military-related psychosocial factors, such as trauma exposure during combat. The combination of these risk factors may potentially contribute to a worsening of symptomatology (Sreenivasan et al., 2013). Research indicates that symptoms of TBI often include presentations similar to PTSD, including hyperarousal, irritability, and difficulty controlling anger, all of which may lead to angry or violent outbursts (Elbogen et al., 2008; Sreenivasan et al., 2013; Tinney & Gerlock, 2014). As such, the compounded symptoms may contribute to more severe levels of psychopathology that have been associated with aggressive behavior. This is demonstrated in a study of veterans with serious mental illness, where the risk of violence was nearly doubled when veterans had both PTSD and TBI diagnoses (Elbogen et al., 2008).

5.2.3.3 Personality Disorders

Current literature suggests that personality traits and disorders are associated with an increased risk for violence. For example, research on risk assessment examines the role psychopathy and other personality disorders have on increasing one's risk for violence toward the self or others (Cooke, 2010). Research has provided evidence of higher prevalent rates of personality disorders in violent offenders and identified personality disorders such as antisocial, borderline, and psychopathy as predictors for future violence at a moderate level (Cooke, 2010). Research has also explored the relationship between different personality disorders and the risk for violence by examining forensic samples (Dunne et al., 2018). The literature currently identifies antisocial as the most frequently observed personality disorder among this population and established that it has been consistently associated with the perpetration of violence (Dunne et al., 2018). Borderline, narcissistic, and paranoid personalities have also been observed at moderate to high rates among forensic samples and have been associated with convictions for serious violent offenses (Dunne et al., 2018).

In a sample of 124,932 Navy personnel who were psychiatrically hospitalized, approximately 27% were diagnosed with a personality disorder (Booth-Kewley & Larson, 2005). Suicidal tendencies and self-harm behaviors, such as intentionally cutting, burning, or tattooing oneself, were strongly correlated with Navy personnel being hospitalized for a personality disorder (Booth-Kewley & Larson, 2005). In addition, interpersonal problems were uniquely predictive of psychiatric hospitalization if the service member was diagnosed with a personality disorder, compared to other mental illnesses (Booth-Kewley & Larson, 2005). It has been estimated that between 2001 and 2007, nearly 26,000 service members were discharged from the military due to a personality disorder diagnosis (Leroux, 2015). Although the circumstances surrounding these separations are unclear, it is suggested that discharge due to a pre-existing personality disorder (e.g., before enlistment) rarely occurs without disciplinary problems (Booth-Kewley & Larson, 2005; Leroux, 2015).

Although limited, some studies have investigated the role that personality traits and disorders play in violence and aggression in military populations. Aggression has previously been correlated to externalizing factors of the Personality Assessment Inventory (PAI), which throughout the literature, consistently includes mania, antisocial features, paranoia, and borderline features (Van Voorhees et al., 2014). Research has suggested that these externalizing factors may be even more strongly correlated to aggressive behavior in military members than PTSD-related symptomatology assessed using the Clinician-Administered PTSD Scale (CAPS; Van Voorhees et al., 2014). As such, personality traits may have a similar, or even greater, influence on service members' risk for violence than other mental health disorders.

A systematic review of studies from the US and UK provides further evidence that personality traits may be especially impactful in service members' risk for violence by discussing how posttraumatic stress symptoms are displayed differently among individuals (MacManus et al., 2015). Although PTSD is an established risk factor for violence among military personnel, there is a wide range of symptom presentations for this disorder. For example, while some individuals internalize symptoms of trauma and are more likely to demonstrate psychological distress through thoughts and moods, others may externalize their experience and express impairment through antisocial behaviors, criminality, and substance use (MacManus et al., 2015). However, some of the literature presents conflicting results. For example, Jakupcak et al. (2007) explored trait anger and hostility of military members and found that although these personality traits were positively associated with combat exposure, results were not significantly related to aggression. Nevertheless, evidence supporting the impact of personality disorders on the risk of violence in the military remains worthy of review.

One of the most frequently studied personality disorders when exploring military members' risk for violence is antisocial personality disorder. As discussed, MacManus et al. (2012) explored the role antisocial traits play concerning aggressive and violent behavior in military members. Specifically, behaviors such as fighting, risky driving, and unlawful behavior prior to enlistment were observed to be associated with violence later in life (MacManus et al., 2012). Among 121 homicides committed by veterans between 2005 and 2007, 39 of the cases demonstrated circumstances of significant antisocial behaviors (Sreenivasan et al., 2013). In a study examining predictive factors associated with IPV among active-duty male Army soldiers, White men who scored high on a measure of negative masculinity, which includes measures of antisocial and narcissistic personality, were more likely to endorse engaging in severe aggression toward their partners (Rosen et al., 2002).

Borderline personality disorder (BPD) has also been explored as it relates to violence in the military. However, studies more often observe this type of personality concerning self-directed violence, rather than violence toward others (Fruhbauerova et al., 2021). These observations are consistent with the diagnostic characteristics of this personality disorder, which often involves self-damaging impulsivity, self-harm, or suicidal behaviors, threats, or gestures (APA, 2013). In a sample of active-duty soldiers who demonstrated significant suicidality, about one-quarter of soldiers met the diagnostic criteria for BPD (Fruhbauerova et al., 2021). In addition, soldiers who demonstrated a higher number of BPD symptoms were more likely to display behaviors of non-suicidal self-injury (Fruhbauerova et al., 2021). Results from another study that examined the relationship between suicidality and personality disorders among soldiers being treated at inpatient and outpatient Army medical sites revealed high levels of antisocial and narcissistic personality symptoms in soldiers who endorsed highly detailed plans of suicide but low desire to carry out those plans (Chu et al., 2017). These findings highlight the importance of exploring the etiology of the individual's suicidal ideation, whether it is circumstantial, a result of comorbid mental illness, or used a manipulation tactic (Chu et al., 2017). Other personalities assessed, such as borderline, avoidant, and dependent, did not demonstrate patterns of a high plan and low desire, which according to the researchers, suggested plans and preparation that pose a higher risk of suicide (Chu et al., 2017).

As discussed, several personality disorders have been linked to either violence toward the self or others among military personnel. Studies have highlighted high prevalence rates for military members to be psychiatrically hospitalized or separated from service due to a personality disorder diagnosis, suggesting significant impairment, disqualification, or even misconduct among these individuals (Booth-Kewley & Larson, 2005; Leroux, 2015). Current literature suggests that personality traits may play an important role in how symptomatology of other relevant disorders, such as PTSD, are expressed (e.g., internalized versus externalized) and related to military members' risk for violence (MacManus et al., 2015). However, future research should aim to investigate the direct relationship between less frequently studied personality disorders, such as paranoid, dependent, and narcissistic personalities, and the risk these disorders contribute to violence in military personnel.

Given the stability of personality traits across the lifespan, special attention should be paid to individuals demonstrating symptoms of personality disorders that have been linked to violent behavior. For example, service members exhibiting behavioral problems typical of antisocial personality disorder during service are likely to continue displaying those behaviors post-discharge. Mental health professionals working in the military may seek to identify and treat active-duty service members who exhibit high-risk personality symptoms to help prevent these individuals from engaging in future violence.

5.2.3.4 Substance Use

Throughout literature that explores the presence of psychiatric disorders and violence, aggressive and violent behaviors have been identified as more prevalent among individuals with a substance use disorder (Coid, 2006; Corrigan & Watson, 2005). Perpetration of violence among clinical patients engaged in treatment for substance abuse is estimated to be two to three times higher than what is typically observed among community samples (Heinz et al., 2015). Military populations experience higher rates of substance use compared to their civilian counterparts (Heinz et al., 2015). Research demonstrates that approximately 10% of veterans seeking services through the VA, and 5–7% of veterans in the community, struggle with an alcohol use disorder (Hoggatt et al., 2017; Seal et al., 2011). In addition, it is estimated that approximately 5% of treatment-seeking veterans, and 1.5% of those in the community, have a substance use disorder that is not related to alcohol (Hoggatt et al., 2017; Seal et al., 2011). These figures are relatively higher compared to percentages seen in civilian populations, with about 4–6% of nonveterans having an alcohol use disorder and 1.4% having a nonalcohol substance use disorder (Hoggatt et al., 2017; Seal et al., 2011). Psychosocial factors, such as influence from military drinking culture and coping with trauma by using substances, are likely to contribute to the elevated prevalence rates and may lead to significant behavioral problems such as violence and aggression (Wainwright et al., 2016).

Substance use among military populations has been well-documented throughout the literature. In addition, the association between substance use and violence in military personnel is substantial. Research has consistently identified alcohol as the most frequently abused substance among this population. In the active force, Judkins et al. (2021) examined alcohol use disorder between 2001 and 2018, identifying 208,870 unique cases. Of those diagnosed, initial diagnoses of new-onset alcohol use disorder occurred most frequently in junior enlisted, Army, White, non-married, male service members, between the ages of 20 and 24 years old. Among a sample of 3247 military personnel seeking VA treatment services, approximately 37% met the criteria for lifetime alcohol use disorder, assessed using the Structured Clinical Interview for DSM Disorders (SCID), followed by cannabis, cocaine, and opioid use disorders (Brancu et al., 2017). Of the same sample, approximately 6% of military members scored in the intermediate range, or above, on the Alcohol Use Disorder Identification Test (AUDIT), indicating a likely or definite alcohol use disorder (Brancu et al., 2017). Participants in the same study were administered the Drug Abuse Screening Tool (DAST), revealing that about 18% of the sample ($N = 595$) suffered from drug abuse, and 4% exhibited drug dependence (Brancu et al., 2017). Similar results were found in a sample of 124 incarcerated veterans, where participants most frequently endorsed alcohol use, followed by marijuana, cocaine, and then heroin use (Saxon et al., 2001). Interestingly, the rate of lifetime use among this sample was consistently higher across all substances if the participant met the criteria for PTSD (Saxon et al., 2001). This finding highlights the importance of understanding the relationship between mental illness, specifically PTSD, and substance use among this population. Previous research suggests that, for both civilian and military populations, it is common for psychiatric symptomatology of PTSD to precede the development of substance use disorders (Bremner et al., 1996; Chilcoat & Breslau, 1998). Thus, it is important to keep in mind the role of PTSD in the etiology and maintenance of substance abuse difficulties, when exploring the impact of misuse on violence in military members (Heinz et al., 2015).

Alcohol is the most frequently researched substance used in the military. Indeed, studies have established a significant association between alcohol misuse and aggression. It is estimated that approximately three-quarters of veterans returning from combat in Vietnam misused alcohol at some point following discharge. Across studies, alcohol use has been significantly associated with aggression and violence among military personnel, especially those with combat experience (MacManus et al., 2015). For example, in one study, active-duty soldiers who screened positive for alcohol abuse were more likely to report severe levels of physical aggression (Gallaway et al., 2012). Research also indicates that alcohol use may exacerbate PTSD-related violence, leading to more physically aggressive acts (MacManus et al., 2015; Van Voorhees et al., 2014). In a study examining the relationship between specific PTSD symptom clusters and overt aggression in veterans, hyperarousal symptoms were related to a greater number of aggressive acts when participants also endorsed alcohol problems (Taft et al., 2007). Consistent with previous literature, this suggests that alcohol misuse may intensify the severity of hyperarousal symptoms, including irritable behavior, angry outbursts, and recklessness (Saladin et al., 1995).

Recent literature has discussed the impact of substance use on veterans' risk for perpetrating different types of violence, such as IPV and non-partner violence. IPV rates, specifically among veterans who use substances, are estimated to range from 42% to 54% (Teten et al., 2009). Although illicit drug use is more strongly related to these types of violence, both drugs and alcohol have been recognized to increase the risk of military personnel committing acts of violence toward another person (Cancio, 2020; Choenni et al., 2017). One study examined the interactions between substance use problems and violence among a sample of veterans seeking VA services for substance use or mental health problems (Sexton et al., 2019). Results indicated a significant, positive relationship between veterans' alcohol consumption and the frequency of physical aggression toward either a partner or non-partner (Sexton et al., 2019). Furthermore, the frequency of heavy drinking was positively associated with aggression severity, indicated by physical injuries sustained by victims. Another study that sought to understand different patterns of violence among veterans seeking substance use treatment found cocaine use to be a significant predictor for violence (Anderson et al., 2017). Consistent with studies examining the impact of comorbid substance use and PTSD symptoms on aggressive behavior, research suggests that rates of IPV have a direct relationship with comorbid alcohol use and PTSD symptoms (MacManus et al., 2015).

As explained, substance use plays a significant role in the perpetration of aggressive and violent behaviors in military personnel. Although noteworthy, the research emphasizes the impact PTSD symptoms have on the relationship between substance abuse and violence, often mediating outcomes (Heinz et al., 2015). As such, the development of prevention and treatment strategies should account for the possibility of psychiatric symptoms exacerbating violent behaviors in military personnel with a history of substance abuse behaviors.

5.3 Summary

This chapter illuminates that violence in the military is a prevalent occurrence, often leading to involvement with the criminal justice system or significant psychosocial consequences for this population (Elbogen et al., 2012a; Taft et al., 2007). In general, military veterans are uniquely represented in the criminal justice system and are typically incarcerated for violent offenses at higher rates when compared to their civilian counterparts (Maruschak et al., 2021). Factors such as aggression, service-related variables, and mental health disorders have all been investigated as they relate to the risk of violence. Each of these factors has been observed as having possible direct or indirect relationships with aggressive and violent behaviors perpetrated by military personnel. The last chapter of the brief will discuss the clinical implications, limitations, and future directions of violent criminal behavior in the military.

References

Afifi, T. O., Taillieu, T., Zamorski, M. A., Turner, S., Cheung, K., & Sareen, J. (2016). Association of child abuse exposure with suicidal ideation, suicide plans, and suicide attempts in military personnel and the general population in Canada. *JAMA Psychiatry, 73*(3), 229–238. https://doi.org/10.1001/jamapsychiatry.2015.2732

Alvarez, L., & Frosch, D. (2009). A focus on violence by Returning G.I.'s. *The New York Times*. https://www.nytimes.com/2009/01/02/us/02veterans.html

American Psychiatric Association. (2013). *Diagnostic and statistical manual of mental disorders* (5th ed.). American Psychiatric Association. https://doi.org/10.1176/appi.books.9780890425596

Anderson, C. A., & Bushman, B. J. (2002). Human aggression. *Annual Review of Psychology, 53*, 27–51. https://doi.org/10.1146/annurev.psych.53.100901.135231

Anderson, R. E., Bonar, E. E., Walton, M. A., Goldstick, J. E., & Ruach, S. M. (2017). A latent profile analysis of aggression and victimization across relationship types among veterans who use substances. *Journal of Studies on Alcohol and Drugs, 78*(4), 597–607. https://doi.org/10.15288/jsad.2017.78.597

Backhaus, A., Gholizadeh, S., Godfrey, K., Pittman, J., & Afari, N. (2016). The many wounds of war: The association of service-related and clinical characteristics with problems with the law in Iraq and Afghanistan veterans. *International Journal of Law and Psychiatry, 49*(Pt B), 205–213. https://doi.org/10.1016/j.ijlp.2016.10.007

Bailie, J. M., Cole, W. R., Ivins, B., Boyd, C., Lewis, S., Neff, J., & Schwab, K. (2015). The experience, expression, and control of anger following traumatic brain injury in a military sample. *Journal of Head Trauma Rehabilitation, 30*(1), 12–20. https://doi.org/10.1097/HTR.0000000000000024

Beckham, J. C., Feldman, M. E., Kirby, A. C., Hertzberg, M. A., & Moore, S. D. (1997). Interpersonal violence and its correlates in Vietnam veterans with chronic posttraumatic stress disorder. *Journal of Clinical Psychology, 53*(8), 859–869. https://doi.org/10.1002/(sici)1097-4679(199712)53:8<859::aid-jclp11>3.0.co;2-j

Benda, B., Rodell, D., & Rodell, L. (2003). Crime among homeless veterans who abuse substances. *Psychiatric Rehabilitation Journal, 26*(4), 332–345. https://doi.org/10.2975/26.2003.332.345

Bennett, D. C., Morris, D. H., Sexton, M. B., Bonar, E. E., & Chermack, S. T. (2018). Associations between posttraumatic stress and legal charges among substance using veterans. *Law and Human Behavior, 42*(2), 135–144. https://doi.org/10.1037/lhb0000268

Black, D. W., Carney, C. P., Peloso, P. M., Woolson, R. F., Letuchy, E., & Doebbeling, B. N. (2005). Incarceration and veterans of the first Gulf war. *Military Medicine, 170*(7), 612–618. https://doi.org/10.7205/milmed.170.7.612

Boal, M. (2011). The kill team: How U.S. soldiers in Afghanistan murdered innocent civilians. *RollingStone*. March 28, 2011. https://www.rollingstone.com/politics/politics-news/the-kill-team-how-u-s-soldiers-in-afghanistan-murdered-innocent-civilians-169793/

Booth-Kewley, S., & Larson, G. E. (2005). Predictors of psychiatric hospitalization in the Navy. *Military Medicine, 170*(1), 87–93. https://doi.org/10.7205/milmed.170.1.874

Booth-Kewley, S., Highfill-McRoy, R. M., Larson, G. E., & Garland, C. F. (2010). Psychosocial predictors of military misconduct. *The Journal of Nervous and Mental Disease, 198*(2), 91–98. https://doi.org/10.1097/NMD.0b013e3181cc45e9

Brancu, M., Wagner, H. R., Morey, R. A., Beckham, J. C., Calhoun, P. S., Tupler, L. A., Marx, C. E., Taber, K. H., Hurley, R. A., Rowland, J., McDonald, S. D., Hoerle, J. M., Moore, S. D., Judler, H. S., Weiner, R. D., VA Mid-Atlantic MIRECC Workgroup, & Fairbank, J. A. (2017). The Post-Deployment Mental Health (PDMH) study and repository: A multi-site study of US Afghanistan and Iraq era veterans. *International Journal of Methods in Psychiatric Research, 26*(3), e1570. https://doi.org/10.1002/mpr.1570

Bremner, J. D., Southwick, S. M., Darnell, A., & Charney, D. S. (1996). Chronic PTSD in Vietnam combat veterans: Course of illness and substance abuse. *The American Journal of Psychiatry, 153*(3), 369–375. https://doi.org/10.1176/ajp.153.3.369

Brignone, E., Fargo, J. D., Blais, R. K., Carter, M. E., Samore, M. H., & Gundlapalli, A. V. (2017). Non-routine discharge from military service: Mental illness, substance use disorders, and suicidality. *American Journal of Preventive Medicine, 52*(5), 557–565. https://doi.org/10.1016/j.amepre.2016.11.015

Brooks Holliday, S., & Pedersen, E. R. (2017). The association between discharge status, mental health, and substance misuse among young adult veterans. *Psychiatry Research, 256*, 428–434. https://doi.org/10.1016/j.psychres.2017.07.011

Cancio, R. (2020). Post-9/11 service era veterans: Intimate partner violence and substance use. *Substance Use & Misuse, 55*(2), 241–251. https://doi.org/10.1080/10826084.2019.1662812

Castillo, D. T., Fallon, S. K., C'de Baca, J., Conforti, K., & Qualls, C. (2002). Anger in PTSD: General psychiatric and gender differences on the BDHI. *Journal of Loss and Trauma, 7*(2), 119–128. https://doi.org/10.1080/153250202753472282

Chilcoat, H. D., & Breslau, N. (1998). Posttraumatic stress disorder and drug disorders: Testing causal pathways. *Archives of General Psychiatry, 55*(10), 913–917. https://doi.org/10.1001/archpsyc.55.10.913

Choenni, V., Hammink, A., & van de Mheen, D. (2017). Association between substance use and the perpetration of family violence in industrialized countries: A systematic review. *Trauma, Violence, & Abuse, 18*(1), 37–50. https://doi.org/10.1177/1524838015589253

Chu, C., Buchman-Schmitt, J. M., Joiner, T. E., & Rudd, M. D. (2017). Personality disorder symptoms and suicidality: Low desire and high plans for suicide in military inpatients and outpatients. *Journal of Personality Disorders, 31*(2), 145–155. https://doi.org/10.1521/pedi_2016_30_241

Coid, J. (2006). Violence and psychiatric morbidity in the national household population of Britain: Public health implications. *The British Journal of Psychiatry, 189*(1), 12–19. https://doi.org/10.1192/bjp.189.1.12

Cooke, D. J. (2010). Personality disorder and violence: Understand violence risk: An introduction to the special section personality disorder and violence. *Journal of Personality Disorders, 24*(5), 539–550. https://doi.org/10.1521/pedi.2010.24.5.539

Corrigan, P. W., & Watson, A. C. (2005). Findings from the National Comorbidity Survey on the frequency of violent behavior in individuals with psychiatric disorders. *Psychiatry Research, 136*(2–3), 153–162. https://doi.org/10.1016/j.psychres.2005.06.005

Coté, I., Heintzman, M., Glancy, G. D., Dufour, M., Hardy, K., & Ward, H. (2020). Veterans behind bars: Examining criminogenic risk factors of veteran incarceration. *Journal of Military, Veteran and Family Health, 6*(S3), 21–30. https://doi.org/10.3138/jmvfh-2020-0003

Currier, J. M., Holland, J. M., Jones, H. W., & Sheu, S. (2014). Involvement in abusive violence among Vietnam veterans: Direct and indirect associations with substance use problems and suicidality. *Psychological Trauma: Theory, Research, Practice, & Policy, 6*(1), 73–82. https://doi-org.ezproxylocal.library.nova.edu/10.1037/a0032973

Department of Defense. (2010). *Protecting the force: Lessons from Fort Hood*. https://sgp.fas.org/eprint/fthood.pdf

Dunne, A. L., Gilbert, F., & Daffern, M. (2018). Elucidating the relationship between personality disorder traits and aggression using the new DSM-5 dimensional–categorical model for personality disorder. *Psychology of Violence, 8*(5), 615–629. https://doi.org/10.1037/vio0000144

Edwards, E. R., Barnes, S., Govindarajulu, U., Geraci, J., & Tsai, J. (2021). Mental health and substance use patterns associated with lifetime suicide attempt, incarceration, and homelessness: A latent class analysis of a nationally representative sample of U.S. veterans. *Psychological Services, 18*(4), 619–631. https://doi.org/10.1037/ser0000488

Elbogen, E. B., Beckham, J. C., Butterfield, M. I., Swartz, M., & Swanson, J. (2008). Assessing risk of violent behavior among veterans with severe mental illness. *Journal of Traumatic Stress, 21*(1), 113–117. https://doi.org/10.1002/jts.20283

Elbogen, E. B., Wagner, H. R., Fuller, S. R., Calhoun, P. S., Kinneer, P. M., Mid-Atlantic Mental Illness Research, Education, and Clinical Center Workgroup, & Beckham, J. C. (2010). Correlates of anger and hostility in Iraq and Afghanistan war veterans. *The American Journal of Psychiatry, 167*(9), 1051–1058. https://doi.org/10.1176/appi.ajp.2010.09050739

Elbogen, E. B., Johnson, S. C., Wagner, H. R., Newton, V. M., Timko, C., Vasterling, J. J., & Beckham, J. C. (2012a). Protective factors and risk modification of violence in Iraq and Afghanistan war veterans. *The Journal of Clinical Psychiatry, 73*(6), e767–e773. https://doi.org/10.4088/JCP.11m07593

Elbogen, E. B., Newton, V. M., Vasterling, J. J., Johnson, S. C., Straits-Troster, K., Wagner, H. R., & Beckham, J. C. (2012b). Criminal justice involvement, trauma, and negative affect in Iraq and Afghanistan war era veterans. *Journal of Consulting and Clinical Psychology, 80*(6), 1097–1102. https://doi.org/10.1037/a0029967

Elbogen, E. B., Wagner, H. R., Brancu, M., Kimbrel, N. A., Naylor, J. C., Swinkels, C. M., Mid-Atlantic, V. A., Workgroup, M. I. R. E. C. C., & Fairbank, J. A. (2018a). Psychosocial risk factors and other than honorable military discharge: Providing healthcare to previously ineligible veterans. *Military Medicine, 183*(9–10), e532–e538. https://doi.org/10.1093/milmed/usx128

Elbogen, E. B., Wagner, H. R., Kimbrel, N. A., Brancu, M., Naylor, J., Graziano, R., & Crawford, E. (2018b). Risk factors for concurrent suicidal ideation and violent impulses in military veterans. *Psychological Assessment, 30*(4), 425–435. https://doi.org/10.1037/pas0000490

Erickson, S., Rosenheck, R., Trestman, R., Ford, J., & Desai, R. (2008). Risk of incarceration between cohorts of veterans with and without mental illness discharged from inpatient units. *Psychiatric Services, 59*(2), 178–183. https://doi.org/10.1176/ps.2008.59.2.178

Fontana, A., & Rosenheck, R. (2005). The role of war-zone trauma and PTSD in the etiology of antisocial behavior. *Journal of Nervous and Mental Disease, 193*(3), 203–209. https://doi.org/10.1097/01.nmd.0000154835.92962.e5

Fruhbauerova, M., DeCou, C. R., Crow, B. E., & Comtois, K. A. (2021). Borderline personality disorder and self-directed violence in a sample of suicidal army soldiers. *Psychological Services, 18*(1), 104–115. https://doi.org/10.1037/ser0000369

Gallaway, M. S., Fink, D. S., Millikan, A. M., & Bell, M. R. (2012). Factors associated with physical aggression among US army soldiers. *Aggressive Behavior, 38*(5), 357–367. https://doi.org/10.1002/ab.21436

GMT. (2012, March 13). Soldier arrested on suspicion of killing his girlfriend. *The Sunday Times*. https://www.thetimes.co.uk/article/soldier-arrested-on-suspicion-of-killing-his-girlfriend-vfppsm67mt2

Greenberg, G. A., & Rosenheck, R. A. (2009). Mental health and other risk factors for jail incarceration among male veterans. *Psychiatric Quarterly, 80*(1), 41–53. https://doi.org/10.1007/s11126-009-9092-8

Heinz, A. J., Makin-Byrd, K., Blonigen, D. M., Reilly, P., & Timko, C. (2015). Aggressive behavior among military veterans in substance use disorder treatment: The roles of posttraumatic stress and impulsivity. *Journal of Substance Abuse Treatment, 50*, 59–66. https://doi.org/10.1016/j.jsat.2014.10.014

Hoggatt, K. J., Lehavot, K., Krenek, M., Schweizer, C. A., & Simpson, T. (2017). Prevalence of substance misuse among U.S. veterans in the general population. *The American Journal on Addictions, 26*, 357–365. https://doi.org/10.1111/ajad.12534

Holliday, S. B., & Pedersen, E. R. (2017). The association between discharge status, mental health, and substance misuse among young adult veterans. *Psychiatry Research, 256*, 428–434. https://doi.org/10.1016/j.psychres.2017.07.011

Hostetter, T. A., Hoffmire, C. A., Forster, J. E., Adams, R. S., Stearns-Yoder, K. A., & Brenner, L. A. (2019). Suicide and traumatic brain injury among individuals seeking Veterans Health Administration services between fiscal years 2006 and 2015. *The Journal of Head Trauma Rehabilitation, 34*(5), E1–E9. https://doi.org/10.1097/HTR.0000000000000489

Iverson, G. L. (2010). Clinical and methodological challenges with assessing mild traumatic brain injury in the military. *The Journal of Head Trauma Rehabilitation, 25*(5), 313–319. https://doi.org/10.1097/HTR.0b013e3181d6f9bd

Jakupcak, M., Conybeare, D., Phelps, L., Hunt, S., Holmes, H. A., Felker, B., Klevens, M., & McFall, M. E. (2007). Anger, hostility, and aggression among Iraq and Afghanistan war veterans reporting PTSD and subthreshold PTSD. *Journal of Traumatic Stress, 20*(6), 945–954. https://doi.org/10.1002/jts.20258

Judkins, J. L., Moore, B. A., Collette, T. L., Hale, J. W., Peterson, A. L., & Morissette, S. B. (2020). Incidence rates of posttraumatic stress disorder over a 17-year period in active duty military service members. *Journal of Traumatic Stress, 33*(6), 994–1006. https://doi.org/10.1002/jts.22558

Judkins, J., Smith, K., Moore, B. A., & Morissette, S. B. (2021). Alcohol use disorder in active duty service members: Incidence rates over a 19-year period. *Substance Abuse, 43*, 1–7. https://doi.org/10.1080/08897077.2021.1941512

Killgore, W. D. S., Cotting, D. I., Thomas, J. L., Cox, A. L., McGurk, D., & Vo, A. H. (2008). Postcombat invincibility: Violent combat experiences are associated with increased risk-taking propensity following deployment. *Journal of Psychiatric Research, 42*(13), 1112–1121. https://doi.org/10.1016/j.jpsychires.2008.01.001

Kornblith, E. S., Yaffe, K., Langa, K. M., & Gardner, R. C. (2020). Prevalence of lifetime history of traumatic brain injury among older male veterans compared with civilians: A nationally representative study. *Journal of Neurotrauma, 37*(24), 2680–2685. https://doi.org/10.1089/neu.2020.7062

Leroux, T. C. (2015). U.S. military discharges and pre-existing personality disorders: A health policy review. *Administration and Policy in Mental Health, 42*(6), 748–755. https://doi.org/10.1007/s10488-014-0611-z

Lovallo, W. R. (2013). Early life adversity reduces stress reactivity and enhances impulsive behavior: Implications for health behaviors. *International Journal of Psychophysiology, 90*, 8–16. https://doi.org/10.1016/j.ijpsycho.2012.10.006

Lucas, K. T., Marcum, C. D., Lucas, P. A., & Blalock, J. (2022). Military veteran involvement with the criminal justice system: A systematic review. *Aggression and Violent Behavior, 66*, 101721. https://doi.org/10.1016/j.avb.2022.101721

MacManus, D., Dean, K., Iversen, A. C., Hull, L., Jones, N., Fahy, T., Wessely, S., & Fear, N. T. (2012). Impact of pre-enlistment antisocial behaviour on behavioural outcomes among U.K. military personnel. *Social Psychiatry and Psychiatric Epidemiology, 47*(8), 1353–1358. https://doi.org/10.1007/s00127-011-0443-z

MacManus, D., Rona, R., Dickson, H., Somaini, G., Fear, N., & Wessely, S. (2015). Aggressive and violent behavior among military personnel deployed to Iraq and Afghanistan: Prevalence and link with deployment and combat exposure. *Epidemiologic Reviews, 37*(1), 196–212. https://doi.org/10.1093/epirev/mxu006

Maruschak, L. M., Bronson, J., & Alper, M. A. (2021). *Survey of prison inmates, 2016: Veterans in prison*. U.S. Department of Justice. Retrieved from https://bjs.ojp.gov/content/pub/pdf/vpspi16st.pdf

McFall, M., Fontana, A., Raskind, M., & Rosenheck, R. (1999a). Analysis of violent behavior in Vietnam combat veteran psychiatric inpatients with posttraumatic stress disorder. *Journal of Traumatic Stress, 12*(3), 501–517. https://doi.org/10.1023/A:1024771121189

McFall, M. E., Wright, P. W., Donovan, D. M., & Raskind, M. (1999b). Multidimensional assessment of anger in Vietnam veterans with posttraumatic stress disorder. *Comprehensive Psychiatry, 40*(3), 216–220. https://doi.org/10.1016/s0010-440x(99)90006-8

Moore, B. A., Hale, W. J., Nabity, P. S., Koehn, T. R., McGeary, D. D., & Peterson, A. L. (2019). A retrospective, epidemiological review of hemiplegic migraines in a military population. *Military Medicine, 184*(11–12), 781–787. https://doi.org/10.1093/milmed/usz040

Moore, B. A., Tison, L. M., Palacios, J. G., Peterson, A. L., & Mysliwiec, V. (2021). Incidence of insomnia and obstructive sleep apnea in active duty United States military service members. *Sleep, 44*(7). https://doi.org/10.1093/sleep/zsab024

Nicholsonn, J. H., Moore, B. A., Dondanville, K., Wheeler, B., & Devoe, E. R. (2020). Examining rates of postpartum depression in active duty military servicewomen. *Journal of Women's Health, 29*(12), 1530–1539. https://doi.org/10.1089/jwh.2019.8172

Noonan, M. E, & Mumola, C. J. (2007). Veterans in state and federal prison, 2004. In *Bureau of justice statistics special report*. U.S. Department of Justice.

Novaco, R. W., & Chembtob, C. M. (2002). Anger and combat related posttraumatic stress disorder. *Journal of Traumatic Stress, 15*, 123–132. https://doi.org/10.1023/A:1014855924072

Orth, U., & Wieland, E. (2006). Anger, hostility, and posttraumatic stress disorder in trauma-exposed adults: A meta-analysis. *Journal of Consulting and Clinical Psychology, 74*(4), 698–706. https://doi.org/10.1037/0022-006X.74.4.698

Reef, J., Diamantopoulou, S., van Meurs, I., Verhulst, F. C., & van der Ende, J. (2011). Developmental trajectories of child to adolescent externalizing behavior and adult DSM-IV disorder: Results of a 24-year longitudinal study. *Social Psychiatry and Psychiatric Epidemiology, 46*(12), 1233–1241. https://doi.org/10.1007/s00127-010-0297-9

Rosen, L. N., Parmley, A. M., Knudson, K. H., & Fancher, P. (2002). Intimate partner violence among married male U.S. army soldiers: Ethnicity as a factor in self-reported perpetration and victimization. *Violence and Victims, 17*(5), 607–622. https://doi.org/10.1891/vivi.17.5.607.33716

Ross, J., Waterhouse-Bradley, B., Contractor, A. A., & Armour, C. (2018). Typologies of adverse childhood experiences and their relationship to incarceration in U.S. military veterans. *Child Abuse & Neglect, 79*, 74–84. https://doi.org/10.1016/j.chiabu.2018.01.023

Russell, P., Judkins, J. L., Blessing, A., Moore, B. A., & Morissette, S. B. (2022). Incidences of anxiety disorders among active duty service members from 1999–2018. *Journal of Anxiety Disorders, 91*, 102608. https://doi.org/10.1016/j.janxdis.2022.102608

Saladin, M. E., Brady, K. T., Dansky, B. S., & Kilpatrick, D. G. (1995). Understanding comorbidity between PTSD and substance use disorder: Two preliminary investigations. *Addictive Behaviors, 20*(5), 643–655. https://doi.org/10.1016/0306-4603(95)00024-7

Saxon, A. J., Davis, T. M., Sloan, K. L., McKnight, K. M., McFall, M. E., & Kivlahan, D. R. (2001). Trauma symptoms of posttraumatic stress disorder, and associated problems among incarcerated veterans. *Psychiatric Services, 52*(7), 959–964. https://doi.org/10.1176/appi.ps.52.7.959

Schein, J., Houle, C., Urganus, A., Cloutier, M., Patterson-Lomba, O., Wang, Y., King, S., Levinson, W., Guérin, A., Lefebvre, P., & Davis, L. L. (2021). Prevalence of post-traumatic stress disorder in the United States: A systematic literature review. *Current Medical Research and Opinion, 37*(12), 2151–2161. https://doi.org/10.1080/03007995.2021.1978417

Schmitt, G. R., & Kerbel, A. (2021). *Federal offenders who served in the armed forces*. United States Sentencing Commission. Retrieved from https://www.ussc.gov/sites/default/files/pdf/research-and-publications/research-publications/2021/20211028_armed-forces.pdf

Seal, K. H., Bertenthal, D., Miner, C. R., Sen, S., & Marmar, C. (2007). Bringing the war back home: Mental health disorders among 103,788 US veterans returning from Iraq and Afghanistan seen at Department of Veterans Affairs facilities. *Archives of Internal Medicine, 167*(5), 476–482. https://doi.org/10.1001/archinte.167.5.476

Seal, K. H., Cohen, G., Waldrop, A., Cohen, B. E., Maguen, S., & Ren, L. (2011). Substance use disorders in Iraq and Afghanistan veterans in VA healthcare, 2001–2010: Implications for screening, diagnosis and treatment. *Drug and Alcohol Dependence, 116*, 93–101. https://doi.org/10.1016/j.drugalcdep.2010.11.027

Sexton, M. B., Davis, A. K., Buchholz, K. R., Winters, J. J., Rauch, S. A., Yzquibell, M., Bonar, E. E., Friday, S., & Chermack, S. T. (2019). Veterans with recent substance use and aggression: PTSD, substance use, and social network behaviors. *Psychological Trauma: Theory, Research, Practice, and Policy, 11*(4), 424–433. https://doi.org/10.1037/trau0000367

Simonoff, E., Elander, J., Holmshaw, J., Pickles, A., Murray, R., & Rutter, M. (2004). Predictors of antisocial personality: Continuities from childhood to adult life. *British Journal of Psychiatry, 184*(2), 118–127. https://doi.org/10.1192/bjp.184.2.118

Smith, D. M., Meruelo, A., Campbell-Sills, L., Sun, X., Kessler, R. C., Ursano, R. J., Jain, S., Stein, M. B., & Army STARRS Team. (2021). Pre-enlistment anger attacks and postenlistment mental disorders and suicidality among US army soldiers. *JAMA Network Open, 4*(9), e2126626. https://doi.org/10.1001/jamanetworkopen.2021.26626

Sreenivasan, S., Garrick, T., McGuire, J., Smee, D. E., Dow, D., & Woehl, D. (2013). Critical concerns in Iraq/Afghanistan war veteran-forensic interface: Combat-related postdeployment criminal violence. *Journal of the American Academy Psychiatry and the Law Online, 41*(2), 263–273.

Taft, C. T., Kaloupek, D. G., Schumm, J. A., Marshall, A. D., Panuzio, J., King, D. W., & Keane, T. M. (2007). Posttraumatic stress disorder symptoms, physiological reactivity, alcohol problems, and aggression among military veterans. *Journal of Abnormal Psychology, 116*(3), 498–507. https://doi.org/10.1037/0021-843X.116.3.498

Taft, C. T., Weatherill, R. P., Woodward, H. E., Pinto, L. A., Watkins, L. E., Miller, M. W., & Dekel, R. (2009). Intimate partner and general aggression perpetration among combat veterans presenting to a posttraumatic stress disorder clinic. *American Journal of Orthopsychiatry, 79*(4), 461–468. https://doi.org/10.1037/a0016657

Teten, A. L., Schumacher, J. A., Bailey, S. D., & Kent, T. A. (2009). Male-to-female sexual aggression among Iraq, Afghanistan, and Vietnam veterans: Co-occurring substance abuse and intimate partner aggression. *Journal of Traumatic Stress, 22*, 307–311. https://doi.org/10.1002/jts.20422

The Defence Analytical Services and Advice. (2010). *Estimating the proportion of offenders supervised by probation trust in England and Wales who are ex-armed forces*. Ministry of Defence. https://assets.publishing.service.gov.uk/government/uploads/system/uploads/attachment_data/file/280539/16-march-2011.pdf

Thomas, J. L., Wilk, J. E., Riviere, L. A., McGurk, D., Castro, C. A., & Hoge, C. W. (2010). Prevalence of mental health problems and functional impairment among active component and National Guard soldiers 3 and 12 months following combat in Iraq. *Archives of General Psychiatry, 67*(6), 614–623. https://doi.org/10.1001/archgenpsychiatry.2010.54

Tinney, G., & Gerlock, A. A. (2014). Intimate partner violence, military personnel, veterans, and their families. *Family Court Review, 52*(3), 400–416. https://doi.org/10.1111/fcre.12100

US Department of Veterans Affairs. (n.d.). *Office of research and development: Traumatic brain injury*. https://www.research.va.gov/topics/tbi.cfm#research3

Van Voorhees, E. E., Dennis, P. A., Elbogen, E. B., Clancy, C. P., Hertzberg, M. A., Beckham, J. C., & Calhoun, P. S. (2014). Personality assessment inventory internalizing and externalizing structure in veterans with posttraumatic stress disorder: Associations with aggression. *Aggressive Behavior, 40*(6), 582–592. https://doi.org/10.1002/ab.21554

Wainwright, V., McDonnell, S., Lennox, C., Shaw, J., & Senior, J. (2016). Soldier, civilian, criminal: Identifying pathways to offending of ex-armed forces personnel in prison. *Psychology, Crime & Law, 22*(8), 741–757. https://doi.org/10.1080/1068316X.2016.1181175

White, M. D., Mulvey, P., & Choate, D. E. (2012). A hero's welcome? Exploring the prevalence and problems of military veterans in the arrestee population. *Justice Quarterly, 29*(2), 258–286. https://doi.org/10.1080/07418825.2011.560890

Chapter 6
Clinical Implications, Limitations, Future Directions, and Conclusions

6.1 Clinical Implications

Violence in the Military Springer Brief focused primarily on suicidality and self-harm, sexual violence, intimate partner and domestic violence, and other violent criminal behavior. In this final chapter, clinical implications, limitations, and future directions of the aforementioned areas are discussed.

6.1.1 Suicide and Self-Harm in the Military

Current research in military suicidal behavior is crucial for informing clinical practice and military leadership awareness. Each contributing factor identified and explained by research allows both clinicians and military leaders to detect, address, and treat suicide risk factors earlier and with greater accuracy. For example, indicators of perceived burdensomeness and thwarted belongingness should be promptly identified and treated, given the evidence that common experiences of military personnel contribute to their acquisition of suicide capability, a known predictor of transition from suicide ideation to a suicide attempt.

Additionally, traditional psychological intervention often focuses on primary emotions such as fear and anxiety. Military personnel experiencing suicidal desire and other psychological disorders would benefit from targeted education and treatment in secondary emotions such as shame and guilt, given their distinct and substantial impact on suicide and psychological functioning among military personnel (Gray et al., 2012; Litz et al., 2009). Shame and guilt in particular frequently result in negative, maladaptive thoughts about the self or a previous action, feelings of worthlessness, withdrawal, self-directed anger and hatred, and exacerbation of post-traumatic stress symptoms. Acceptance and commitment therapy, adaptive

M. T. Baker et al., *Violence in the Military*, SpringerBriefs in Psychology,
https://doi.org/10.1007/978-3-031-26883-0_6

disclosure, and self-forgiveness interventions can be effective for restructuring negative self-schemas, improving psychological flexibility, developing coping skills, and increasing self-compassion and self-esteem in ways traditional PTSD treatment does not (Vermetten & Jetly, 2018).

When examining these constructs, shame—for example—is highly associated with social withdrawal (Tangney et al., 2007; Taylor, 2015); thus, group therapy could be beneficial for promoting social reconnection and re-establishing self-worth. Because behavior is more easily modifiable than the self, it could be argued that guilt is easier to address and treat than shame. Through treatment, an individual can shift blame from themselves toward their behavior, enabling them to feel a greater sense of worth and control. Like shame, guilt can be targeted by both cognitive- and emotion-based therapeutic approaches to address behavior-based maladaptive thoughts and associated distress. In the case of combat veterans and trauma survivors experiencing moral injury, acceptance and commitment therapy may be particularly helpful in actively accepting what has been done and skillfully managing related thoughts and emotions. Further, Trauma-Informed Guilt Reduction Therapy (TrIGR) has been developed to fill gaps in traditional PTSD intervention and specifically addresses emotional and cognitive sequelae of shame, guilt, and moral injury, but is still undergoing preliminary clinical trials to confirm efficacy (Capone et al., 2021).

As previously stated, the association between mental health disorders and suicidal behavior is vastly nuanced. Research indicates that diagnosis alone does not result in service member death by suicide or even attempt, but rather psychological symptoms such as hopelessness, shame, guilt, withdrawal, and negative cognitive and affective states. Thus, relevant symptoms should be targeted in clinical assessment and intervention over the broader construct of diagnosis. For example, Service Member A presents with a depressed mood, weight gain, insomnia, anhedonia, and suicidal ideation. Traditional treatment may utilize cognitive-behavioral strategies such as behavioral activation and cognitive restructuring to increase Service Member A's activity and challenge thoughts regarding their current state. While these are helpful strategies for Service Member A's overall health and well-being, their complete isolation from their unit and family members, strong beliefs that they did such a terrible thing that every person they know would be better off without them, and tolerance to physical pain are not directly or promptly addressed, thus subjecting them to prolonged suicidal ideation and increased risk of transitioning from ideation to suicide attempt.

6.1.2 Military Sexual Violence: Culture

Sexual violence has been a pervasive issue in the US military for centuries; however, in the past decade, politicians and high-ranking officials are becoming more aware and taking action. Sexual trauma occurs nearly twice as frequently in military populations than in civilian populations and is largely attributed to the environment and culture (Schmid, 2010). Military culture has been found to exacerbate feelings of hopelessness and helplessness survivors experience due to systemic difficulties survivors encounter before and after reporting sexual violence (Castro et al., 2015; Northcut & Kienow, 2014).

Castro et al. (2015) attribute the prevalence of sexual assault to the hyper-masculinity found within the military. They found various cultural aspects that increase the risk of MST, such as cultural acceptance, alcohol use, and hyper-masculinity. Regarding cultural acceptance, they referred to the "code of silence" that is perceived through the chain of command. Specifically, the "code of silence" discourages an open reporting climate, therefore, instilling fear of retaliation and negative repercussions among service members. The "code of silence" phenomenon has been witnessed in the military culture around the globe. Indeed, New Zealand's Defence Force reported the code of silence has been perpetuated through a "lack of transparency and accountability" (Fisher, 2020) with military culture being one of the largest factors in rates of sexual violence.

Additionally, alcohol use and misuse have been prevalent in military settings for decades and is linked to an increased risk of sexual violence (Castro et al., 2015). Further, they found that hyper-masculinity reinforces traditional, outdated gender stereotypes. This creates an "us vs. them" mindset, leaving servicewomen to feel scrutinized and sexualized by their peers (Castro et al., 2015). Although the military as a whole is taking steps to provide support to survivors, the innate fear of repercussions and stigmatization remains pervasive (Northcut & Kienow, 2014). Thus, when treating a survivor of MST, it is crucial to recognize the impact of the military culture and the contributing factors to their trauma experience.

6.1.2.1 Treatment Considerations

Military psychologists face complex ethical dilemmas and are often required to evaluate a survivor's mental health. Confidentiality and conflicting dual roles play a substantial part in military psychologists' daily tasks; however, research indicates these factors are crucial to the development of a therapeutic alliance. Little research currently focuses on the intricacies of treating MST, which is typically treated as PTSD. The Veterans Health Administration (VHA) recognizes the pervasive nature of MST, and in turn, the VA system employs MST coordinators to assist in the mental and physical healthcare of veterans that have experienced MST (United States Department of Veterans Affairs, 2019). Considering this is the closest current comparison, the US Department of Veterans Affairs (2019) lists the evidence-based practices as prolonged exposure, cognitive processing therapy, cognitive behavioral therapy, interpersonal therapy, acceptance and commitment therapy, motivation enhancement therapy, and dialectical behavior therapy. Each type of therapy listed has shown positive mental health outcomes for survivors of MST, however, focuses on the mental health diagnosis associated with MST. Military sexual violence is classified as an *experience* and is not currently a diagnosis, therefore, cannot be treated as such. Additionally, these evidence-based practices can be found at

Veterans Affairs and must be carried out by a licensed mental health professional. Other forms of treatment, such as spiritual or community-based support, may be considered helpful to an individual, however, are not currently evidence-based practices with empirical efficacy.

6.1.3 Intimate Partner and Domestic Violence Among Military Populations

Understanding the context of violence can help tailor services to meet the varying needs of individuals impacted by IPV. It is worth noting that violence within any context can be dangerous and potentially lethal. The purpose of determining the context is not intended to minimize risk, danger, or excuse IPV-related behavior. Instead, context can inform decisions related to perpetrator disposition and victim safety and help determine appropriate intervention and safety planning. Johnson's typologies, for example, can inform screening and identification protocols, service responses, and interventions (Johnson & Leone, 2005; Johnson, 2010, 2017). Screening and assessments should be used to identify the presence of co-occurring conditions and risk factors that may increase an individual's risk for IPV perpetration.

When service members are victims of IPV, the resulting physical and mental trauma may negatively impact their ability to deploy or serve in their intended capacity. Additionally, the actions and imposed sanctions of military commanders can be influential in IPV intervention by establishing a precedent where victims feel safe reporting IPV, and perpetrators are held accountable.

6.1.4 Violent Criminal Behavior

Several important clinical implications should be considered regarding mitigating violence in military populations. First, the association between aggressive traits and violence must not be overlooked. The review of current literature, as it relates to military personnel, suggests aggression is a substantial risk factor for the perpetration of violence. As such, it is essential to provide both active-duty service members and veterans who display these traits strategies for coping with aggression. As a preventative measure, implementing more adaptive coping mechanisms that are geared toward managing aggressive impulses (e.g., DBT skills of emotion regulation) throughout military training may allow service members to begin practicing these skills before their aggression reaches a level of dangerousness.

Service-related factors should also be considered among the clinical implications of this report. The behaviors, attitudes, and life experiences that service members possess before joining the service can be informative in predicting and mitigating violence. Screening for antisocial behaviors, childhood abuse and trauma, and other negative life events before joining the service may inform the care of new service members. Referring service members to individual psychotherapy, group therapy, or other social support groups as needed can help reduce future violence by targeting relevant risk factors they have acquired in their past histories. Although the direct impact of deployment and combat exposure on the risk for violence is difficult to ascertain, these factors often interact with others to produce potentially dangerous outcomes. As such, thorough and consistent debriefing strategies should be employed throughout their career for service members who are deployed, were exposed to combat, or have faced traumatizing events while serving. Immediate and constant processing of these events may help reduce the chance that these challenging experiences and adversities will exacerbate the effects of other risk factors for violence. In addition, a review of the literature on discharge deposition as a risk factor for violence highlights the importance of providing affordable and accessible mental healthcare to all service members following discharge. Implementing more effective strategies for assisting service members with transitioning into civilian life, regardless of status at discharge, can help alleviate some of the psychosocial stressors (e.g., homelessness and unemployment associated with other than honorable or dishonorable discharge status) that military populations often face, which may contribute to violence.

Finally, the prevalence of mental illness among service members and veterans and the relationship between specific diagnoses and violence (e.g., PTSD, TBI, antisocial personality disorder, substance use disorders) calls for a need to provide preventative interventions for military personnel experiencing psychiatric symptoms. Accurate diagnostic assessment becomes an important strategy to consider when attempting to mitigate violence among military populations. Identifying emerging symptoms of disorders that are readily linked to violence will help inform early preventative interventions to reduce the risk of violence to the self or others. Implementing intervention strategies throughout service and following discharge, especially while transiting to civilian life, may assist service members and veterans in maintaining stability in their mental health, before their symptoms reach a level that could contribute to violence.

6.2 Limitations

6.2.1 Suicide and Self-Harm in the Military

Despite decades of research targeting suicidal risk factors and behavior among US service members, limitations remain in current research. For example, the association between deployment and suicidal behavior remains unclear. A better definition of terms related to deployment, including specific combat experiences and exposure to death and killing, has been suggested to improve the quality and accuracy of deployment and suicidality research (Bryan, 2015). Additionally, there is limited research regarding the rapid escalation of symptoms which may transition an individual from suicide ideation to active suicidal behavior given the short timeframe in which such escalation occurs (Yamaguchi et al., 2021). Further, it is difficult to retrospectively identify risk factors which separate those individuals who complete suicide and those who do not given that individuals who die by suicide are no longer available for interviewing. The psychological autopsy conducted by Nock et al. (2017) proved to be a useful source of retrospective information on suicide decedents; thus, methods used in the study should be replicated in the future. Lastly, stigma related to mental health treatment in the military remains a barrier to reporting mental health symptoms and receiving appropriate care. Further research into reducing stigma, improving treatment seeking behaviors, and reducing barriers to mental health treatment would be useful in early detection and prevention of suicidal behavior.

6.2.2 Military Sexual Violence

A magnitude of the current literature on military sexual trauma highlights prevalence and areas for future consideration. There is a dearth of literature examining the implications of reporting and the potential for underreporting, thus, making it difficult to obtain accurate data on the occurrence of MST. Considering the cultural barriers and stigmatization of MST, many service members may not attempt to report, which impacts known prevalence rates as well as the resource allocation and human capital support provided. Research is currently lacking on the impact of military culture on survivors of MST and their mental and physical health outcomes. Based on preliminary data and anecdotal evidence, this is an important factor to further investigate.

Finally, current literature typically focuses on servicewomen's experience of MST and excludes servicemen. Prevalence rates indicate men do experience MST, albeit, at a different rate than servicewomen. The lack of attention to the experiences of male service members is likely to perpetuate stigma and reduce reporting. Research examining gender differences and the potential stigmatization that occurs is warranted. Much of the current literature focuses on long-term health outcomes and prevalence rates. While this literature helps provide context to such a vast and complex topic, treatment efficacy and effectiveness for MST survivors are needed to improve current clinical practice and decrease the long-term health impacts of MST on service members.

6.2.3 Intimate Partner and Domestic Violence Among Military Populations

Several factors complicate the direct comparison of military and nonmilitary Intimate Partner Violence/Domestic Violence (IPV/DV) datasets, including process differences between how DoD and nonmilitary data are reported, collected, and aggregated. Additionally, not all research differentiates between IPV and violence directed toward other family members. Most of the research on IPV in general, and within the military, utilizes self-report measures or incidents of IPV, which is likely underreported as compared to the actual prevalence of IPV.

6.2.4 Violent Criminal Behavior in the Military

Violent criminal behavior research does not go without limitation. For example, the quantitative data about incarcerated veterans that was presented was readily drawn from a 2016 Bureau of Justice statistics report (Maruschak et al., 2021). Importantly, this report only addressed statistics of incarcerated male veterans. Unfortunately, data on justice-involved female veterans was not provided. Additionally, incarceration facilities often report veteran status if this is self-disclosed. When considered through the lens of identity dissonance, many veterans with a strong sense of honor or service may experience shame or guilt related to their actions and not disclose their veteran status, thereby contributing to an underreporting of the numbers of justice-involved veterans. As such, future studies should aim to explore the rate of incarceration and types of crimes female veteran offenders commit to contribute to a more inclusive understanding of violent criminal offending among military members. In addition, the discussion of mental health as a risk factor for violence among military members predominantly focuses on specific diagnoses (e.g., PTSD, TBI, personality disorders, and substance use disorders) that have been previously associated with violent behavior, and less is known about mental health diagnoses that are less frequently associated with violence. Future research should investigate the impact that other mental health diagnoses (e.g., depression, anxiety, bipolar disorder, schizophrenia) may have on community resource availability as well as the influence of these contributors on military members' risk for violent behavior.

6.3 Future Directions

6.3.1 Suicide and Self-Harm in the Military

While the current research base has been instrumental in developing clinical tools and preventative efforts in place today, consistently elevated rates of suicide among military personnel indicate that current understanding and treatment of suicidal behavior remains limited. To better understand the psychological mechanisms by which traumatic events and mental health diagnoses influence service members to attempt or die by suicide, more research into the risk factors identified in this chapter is crucial. Specifically, prospective research on suicidal behavior is lacking, which limits our ability to determine the directionality of factors related to suicidal ideation and attempt. A greater understanding of these mechanisms would allow clinicians to refine and enhance existing interventions, or even develop novel methods to address previously unknown psychological experiences and consequences of war. Prevention and intervention of service member's suicidal behavior are necessary to maintain operational readiness. Additionally, and most importantly, the development and enhancement of public health awareness within the military commonly disseminate into civilian healthcare. Improving suicide prevention and intervention and reducing service member suicide rates allows for a better quality of life, increased safety, and well-being, and facilitates greater levels of happiness and health among US military members, their families, their communities, and US citizens as a whole.

6.3.2 Military Sexual Violence

Due to the extensive processes and policies of federal institutions such as the military, it is understandable why change and progress require an abundance of time. Despite this difficulty, it should be recognized that MST prevalence and health impacts on service members have been problematic for decades. Globally, sexual violence in the military is one of the highest reported causes of posttraumatic stress disorder and other health concerns (Morgan, 2020). With the correlation between prior exposure to sexual violence and revictimization increasing, education and awareness is at the forefront of future directions.

While research has expanded exponentially in the past decades, gaps in the literature remain. As sexual violence has been observed globally, more research is required to glean accurate prevalence rates and make appropriate adjustments in reporting requirements. Additionally, more focus should be placed on recognizing the long-term health impacts of MST, the prevalence of sexual hazing and MST in servicemen, and reporting deficiencies.

Future research should also focus specifically on developing a standardized mental health evaluation for sexual violence victims. This research can assist in the reform of the current protocol and eliminate ethical challenges. Evidence suggests that individuals report secondary traumatization through ethical violations and systematic disregard for sexual violence within the military (Mengeling et al., 2014; Myers, 2017). Approaches and procedures which focus on the victim, their experience, and their health would likely have positive results; however, until more awareness and attention are brought to this issue, no change will be implemented. In current situations, the victims of sexual assault are not only talking to a psychologist but also a fellow soldier who likely knows the assailant well. By requiring a third-party evaluation for soldiers alleging victimization and having set protocols for post-MST evaluations, survivors would have a more objective and comprehensive experience when seeking health and occupational assistance following sexual violence.

Lastly, in combination with further research and changes in evaluation, military psychologists should be trained on the broad impacts of victimization. Due to the unique culture and embedded military identity, survivors tend to react to trauma in a much different way than civilians (Mengeling et al., 2014; Gilbred, 2017). Thus, highlighting a need to train psychologists working with veterans and active-duty military specifically on how to handle cases of MST. Much work remains to advance the current approaches outside the military and meaningfully examine how such approaches could be adapted to the military, to help develop a unique method that considers the dynamic created between military psychologists and sexual violence victims.

6.3.3 Intimate Partner and Domestic Violence Among Military Populations

It is apparent that numerous factors likely increase prevalence rates of both intimate partner and domestic violence. Future research should focus on increasing transparency surrounding this problem, enhancing the understanding of the context of violence, and its impact on victim's mental and physical health. Factors unique to military involvement need to be explored, as they may exacerbate risks for perpetrators and victims of IPV and should be given further attention when determining prevention and intervention strategies.

6.3.4 Violent Criminal Behavior in the Military

Based on the conclusions drawn from the chapter on violent criminal behavior, areas warranting further investigation are recognized. For example, future research may wish to explore the relevance of symptom onset regarding psychiatric disorders that are frequently associated with violence. If researchers can better understand the relationship between symptom onset and perpetration of violence, then relevant interventions can be implemented to reduce the severity or course of emotional or behavioral disturbances. This is important when considering the impact mental health difficulties have on service members pre-, during, and post-service. Some service members may demonstrate difficulties pre-enlistment, which puts them at a disadvantage in being accepted into a certain military branch or completing basic training. Alternatively, service members may begin to display emotional or behavioral impairments during service, which could lead to a discharge type other than honorable, or even dishonorable if they commit a conduct offense. Service members who obtain a dishonorable discharge are likely to experience even greater difficulty transitioning to civilian life, especially when it comes to finding employment opportunities. This increase in psychosocial stress is likely to amplify the risk of violence. As such, identifying the relationship between symptom onset and violence may be beneficial for mitigating the risk of negative psychosocial consequences.

Another area worthy of additional research is exploring more thoroughly the complexity that is added to psychiatric diagnoses when there is co-occurring substance use, and the contribution this has to violence risk in military populations. Substance abuse and substance use disorders have been established as significant risk factors for justice-involvement in veteran populations and are deserving of further exploration (Benda et al., 2003; Cancio, 2020; Elbogen et al., 2012; Erickson et al., 2008; Lucas et al., 2022; Van Voorhees et al., 2014). Some studies suggest that substance use may exacerbate the risk of aggression and violence exhibited by veterans who are diagnosed with comorbid mental illness (Van Voorhees et al., 2014). However, the directionality of the relationship between substance use may be complicated if the veteran is also presenting with other symptoms of mental illness that are associated with violent behavior. As such, research that further investigates the onset of substance use and psychiatric symptoms will contribute to a clearer understanding of the developmental timeline of these risk factors. This could potentially assist mental health professionals with intervening before the development of co-occurring emotional or behavioral problems.

Finally, the research discussed in this paper provides a rationale for identifying protective factors specific to the development of the aforementioned risk factors of violence among military populations. Once identified, mental health professionals can help service members recognize, obtain, and utilize effective protective factors and coping mechanisms, which may help reduce the risk of violence to themselves or others in the future.

6.4 Conclusions

The global war on terrorism resulted in a continual involvement of the United States (US) military and allied nations from 2001 to 2021. While the training and experiences of service members are essential to national security, 20 years of conflict and ongoing military operations greatly impacted both the service member and their families. The requirement and expectation of constant readiness for or exposure to organized violence may contribute to the expression of violence outside of the military through the exacerbation of aggressive traits. The impact of the aforementioned training and experiences on service members' mental health, behavior, and propensity toward non-combat-related violence. This brief examined several relevant areas with US military, families, veterans, and allied forces. These areas included suicidality and self-harm, sexual violence, intimate partner and domestic violence, and other violent criminal behavior. The clinical implications, limitations, and future directions of these aforementioned areas were discussed above.

Most recent suicide statistics within the US military remain elevated despite governmental, organizational, and community prevention efforts. Many personal and organizational factors contribute to suicidal behavior in service members, and currently, there are several theories explaining the development and maintenance of suicidal behavior. Greater accuracy in the detection of suicide precedents will enable military leaders and healthcare providers to identify at-risk service members sooner and enact more effective prevention and intervention tactics. Similarly, enhanced resiliency can not only reduce risk of suicide but also optimize operational performance and mission readiness.

Miliary sexual trauma (MST) is a pervasive issue throughout the US military that requires immediate, effective policy change and empirical attention. Survivors of military sexual violence face challenges unlike those in civilian life, including revictimization, difficulty reporting, repeated exposure to their abuser, and feelings of helplessness. These factors are unique to military culture due to the commitment to service, rank, and formality required in service. Further, military culture appears to have a large role in exacerbating the trauma experience of survivors. Service members are provided very few reporting opportunities, each providing unique challenges. When service members choose to report sexual assault, they may complete either Unrestricted or Restricted reporting. Due to the complexities and restrictions of these reporting options, this decision must be fully informed and made amid their traumatic experience.

Throughout the MST research, it is clear there are negative outcomes for the mental and physical health of survivors. Literature indicated survivors have an increased risk of chronic disease, organ failure, obesity, and sexual dysfunction (e.g., Forkus et al., 2021; McCall-Hosenfeld et al., 2009; Suris & Lind, 2008). Psychologically, they suffer from higher rates of cumulative trauma resulting in PTSD, depression, suicide, and substance use (e.g., Calhoun et al., 2018; Kelly et al., 2011; Kimerling et al., 2016). Survivors no longer feel a sense of identity in the military and often feel disconnected from peers and social support networks. This leads to a loss of professional and personal identity, feelings of helplessness and hopelessness, and resentment toward their country (Castro et al., 2015; Northcut & Kienow, 2014; Schmid, 2010). Survivors face challenges regarding reporting options and overall outcomes that are unique to military culture. Continued research would provide insight into the high rates of personality disorders given to MST survivors and enhance current protocols and policies that are lacking. It is the responsibility of researchers to help understand what challenges continue to emerge and how to best improve the treatment and evaluation of MST.

It is apparent that intimate partner and domestic violence is evident among military populations. While numerous factors likely increase prevalence rates, there is little being done to focus on the prevention of its perpetration. Within the military culture, the values of strength and power likely decrease one's ability to admit IPV fault or victimization. Raising awareness of the veracity of this problem enables better understanding of the context of violence and its impact on victim's mental and physical health.

Violence in the military is a prevalent occurrence, often leading to involvement with the criminal justice system or significant psychosocial consequences for this population (Elbogen et al., 2012; Taft et al., 2007). In general, military veterans are uniquely represented in the criminal justice system and are typically incarcerated for violent offenses at higher rates when compared to their civilian counterparts (Maruschak et al., 2021). High-profile and deadly events, such as the shootings at

Fort Hood, hastened the need for understanding violent behavior among military personnel. As such, factors such as aggression, service-related variables, and mental health disorders have all been investigated as they relate to the risk of violence. Each of these factors has been observed as having possible direct or indirect relationships with aggressive and violent behaviors perpetrated by military personnel. Attaining a better understanding of these relationships can greatly contribute to the enhancement of intervention strategies and establishing of prevention methods.

Non-combat-related violence including suicidality, sexual violence, intimate partner violence, and violent criminal behavior was examined in this brief. Factors contributing to the perpetration of violence and subtypes were also reviewed including personality traits (i.e., aggression), the military life cycle, interpersonal dynamics, and mental health. The full extent of the impact of the training and deployment experiences on service members' mental health, behavior, and propensity toward non-combat-related violence may be never known. However, identifying and addressing factors enabling or exacerbating violent behavior are crucial for the long-term health and safety of US service members, families, veterans, our military allies, and the communities in which they live.

References

Benda, B., Rodell, D., & Rodell, L. (2003). Crime among homeless veterans who abuse substances. *Psychiatric Rehabilitation Journal, 26*(4), 332–345. https://doi.org/10.2975/26.2003.332.345

Bryan, C. J. (2015). On deployment and military suicide risk. *JAMA Psychiatry, 72*(9), 949–950.

Calhoun, P. S., Schry, A. R., Dennis, P. A., Wagner, H. R., Kimbrel, N. A., Bastian, L. A., Beckham, J. C., Kudler, H., & Straits-Tröster, K. (2018). The association between military sexual trauma and use of VA and non-VA health care services among female veterans with military service in Iraq or Afghanistan. *Journal of Interpersonal Violence, 33*(15), 2439–2464. https://doi.org/10.1177/0886260515625909

Cancio, R. (2020). Post-9/11 service era veterans: Intimate partner violence and substance use. *Substance Use & Misuse, 55*(2), 241–251. https://doi.org/10.1080/10826084.2019.1662812

Capone, C., Norman, S. B., Haller, M., Davis, B., Shea, M. T., Browne, K., et al. (2021). Trauma informed guilt reduction (TrIGR) therapy for guilt, shame, and moral injury resulting from trauma: Rationale, design, and methodology of a two-site randomized controlled trial. *Contemporary Clinical Trials, 101*, 106251. https://doi.org/10.1016/j.cct.2020.106251

Castro, C. A., Kintzle, S., Schuyler, A. C., Lucas, C. L., & Warner, C. H. (2015). Sexual assault in the military. *Current Psychiatry Report, Military Mental Health, 17*, 1–13. https://doi.org/10.1007/s11920-015-0596-7

Elbogen, E. B., Johnson, S. C., Wagner, H. R., Newton, V. M., Timko, C., Vasterling, J. J., & Beckham, J. C. (2012). Protective factors and risk modification of violence in Iraq and Afghanistan War veterans. *The Journal of Clinical Psychiatry, 73*(6), e767–e773. https://doi.org/10.4088/JCP.11m07593

Erickson, S., Rosenheck, R., Trestman, R., Ford, J., & Desai, R. (2008). Risk of incarceration between cohorts of veterans with and without mental illness discharged from inpatient units. *Psychiatric Services, 59*(2), 178–183. https://doi.org/10.1176/ps.2008.59.2.178

Fisher, D. (2020, July 15). *New review finds a 'code of silence' problems dooming plan to eliminate sexual violence in our military*. New Zealand Herald. https://www.nzherald.co.nz/nz/new-review-finds-a-code-of-silence-among-the-problems-dooming-plan-to-eliminate-sexual-violence-in-our-military/7AVTOA25GXOUAKLKKPBTHL5MUE/

Forkus, S. R., Weiss, N. H., Goncharenko, S., Mammay, J., Church, M., & Contractor, A. A. (2021). Military sexual trauma and risky behaviors: A review. *Trauma, Violence, & Abuse, 22*(4), 976–993. https://doi.org/10.1177/1524838019897338

Gilbred, K. (2017, July). *Challenging military sexual violence.* http://nlgmltf.org/military-law-library/publications/memos/military-sexual-violence/

Gray, M. J., Schorr, Y., Nash, W., Lebowitz, L., Amidon, A., Lansing, A., & Litz, B. T. (2012). Adaptive disclosure: An open trial of a novel exposure-based intervention for service members with combat-related psychological stress injuries. *Behavior Therapy, 43*(2), 407–415. https://doi.org/10.1016/j.beth.2011.09.001

Johnson, M. P. (2010). *Typology of domestic violence intimate terrorism, violent resistance, and situational couple violence.* Northeastern University Press.

Johnson, M. P. (2017). A personal social history of a typology of intimate partner violence. *Journal of Family Theory & Review, 9*(2), 150–164. https://doi.org/10.1111/jftr.12187

Johnson, M. P., & Leone, J. M. (2005). The differential effects of intimate terrorism and situational couple violence. *Journal of Family Issues, 26*(3), 322–349. https://doi.org/10.1177/0192513x04270345

Kelly, U., Skelton, K., Patel, M., & Bradley, B. (2011). More than military sexual trauma: Interpersonal violence, PTSD, and mental health in women veterans. *Research in Nursing & Health, 34*, 457–467. https://doi.org/10.1002/nur.20453

Kimerling, R., Makin-Byrd, K., Louzon, S., Ignacio, R. V., & McCarthy, J. F. (2016). Military sexual trauma and suicide mortality. *American Journal of Prevalent Medicine, 50*(6), 684–691. https://doi.org/10.1016/j.amepre.2015.10.019

Litz, B. T., Stein, N., Delaney, E., Lebowitz, L., Nash, W. P., Silva, C., & Maguen, S. (2009). Moral injury and moral repair in war veterans: A preliminary model and intervention strategy. *Clinical Psychology Review, 29*(8), 695–706. https://doi.org/10.1016/j.cpr.2009.07.003

Lucas, K. T., Marcum, C. D., Lucas, P. A., & Blalock, J. (2022). Military veteran involvement with the criminal justice system: A systematic review. *Aggression and Violent Behavior, 66*, 101721. https://doi.org/10.1016/j.avb.2022.101721

Maruschak, L. M., Bronson, J., & Alper, M. A. (2021). *Survey of prison inmates, 2016: Veterans in prison.* U.S. Department of Justice. Retrieved from https://bjs.ojp.gov/content/pub/pdf/vpspi16st.pdf

McCall-Hosenfeld, J. S., Liebschutz, J. M., Spiro, A., & Seaver, M. R. (2009). Sexual assault in the military and its impact of sexual satisfaction in women veterans: A proposed model. *Journal of Women's Health, 18*(6), 901–909. https://doi.org/10.1089/jwh.2008.0987

Mengeling, M. A., Booth, B. M., Torner, J. C., & Salder, A. G. (2014). Reporting sexual assault in the military: Who reports and why most servicewomen don't. *American Journal of Preventative Medicine, 47*(1), 17–25. https://doi.org/10.1016/j.amepre.2014.03.001

Morgan, L. (2020). Understanding sexual offences in UK military and veteran populations: Delineating the offences and setting research priorities. *BMJ Military Health, 168*, 146–149. http://orcid.org/0000-0001-8422-9571

Myers, M. (2017, August 07). *Former soldiers with service-connected sexual trauma can apply for discharge upgrades.* https://www.armytimes.com/news/your-army/2017/02/03/former-soldiers-with-service-connected-sexual-trauma-can-apply-for-discharge-upgrades/

Nock, M. K., Dempsey, C. L., Aliaga, P. A., Brent, D. A., Heeringa, S. G., Kessler, R. C., et al. (2017). Psychological autopsy study comparing suicide decedents, suicide ideators, and propensity score matched controls: Results from the study to assess risk and resilience in service members (Army STARRS). *Psychological Medicine, 47*(15), 2663–2674. https://doi.org/10.1017/S0033291717001179

Northcut, T. B., & Kienow, A. (2014). The trauma trifecta of military sexual trauma: A case study illustrating the integration of mind and body in clinical work with survivors of MST. *Clinical Social Work Journal, 42*(3), 247–259. https://doi.org/10.1007/s10615-014-0479-0

Schmid, M. N. (2010). Combating different enemy: Proposals to change the culture of sexual assault in the military. *Villanova Law Review, 55*(2), 475–508.

Suris, A., & Lind, L. (2008). Military sexual trauma: A review of prevalence and associated health consequences in veterans. *Trauma, Violence, & Abuse, 9*(4), 250–269. https://doi.org/10.1177/1524838008324419

Taft, C. T., Kaloupek, D. G., Schumm, J. A., Marshall, A. D., Panuzio, J., King, D. W., & Keane, T. M. (2007). Posttraumatic stress disorder symptoms, physiological reactivity, alcohol problems, and aggression among military veterans. *Journal of Abnormal Psychology, 116*(3), 498–507. https://doi.org/10.1037/0021-843X.116.3.498

Tangney, J. P., Stuewig, J., & Mashek, D. J. (2007). Moral emotions and moral behavior. *Annual Review of Psychology, 58*, 345–372. https://doi-org.ezproxylocal.library.nova.edu/10.1146/annurev.psych.56.091103.070145

Taylor, T. F. (2015). The influence of shame on posttrauma disorders: Have we failed to see the obvious? *European Journal of Psychotraumatology, 6*(1), 28847. https://doi.org/10.3402/ejpt.v6.28847

United States Department of Veterans Affairs. (2019, January 7). *MST-related treatment and support resources for veterans*. https://www.mentalhealth.va.gov/msthome/treatment.asp

Van Voorhees, E. E., Dennis, P. A., Elbogen, E. B., Clancy, C. P., Hertzberg, M. A., Beckham, J. C., & Calhoun, P. S. (2014). Personality assessment inventory internalizing and externalizing structure in veterans with posttraumatic stress disorder: Associations with aggression. *Aggressive Behavior, 40*(6), 582–592. https://doi.org/10.1002/ab.21554

Vermetten, E., & Jetly, R. (2018). A critical outlook on combat-related PTSD: Review and case reports of guilt and shame as drivers for moral injury. *Military Behavioral Health, 6*(2), 156–164. https://doi.org/10.1080/21635781.2018.1459973

Yamaguchi, C., Parekh, B., & Koritzky, G. (2021). Military culture and its impact on mental health and stigma. *Journal of Community Engagement and Scholarship, 13*(4), 10.

Index

A
Abuse, 7, 11, 19, 20, 22, 23, 25, 26, 29, 33, 34, 36–43, 50–53, 55, 56, 58, 59, 65–67, 78, 84
Abuser, 19, 24, 26, 27, 29, 33, 34, 37–39, 85
Aggression, 2, 33, 35, 43, 51–57, 59–67, 78, 84, 86
Allies, 1, 13, 86

C
Criminal behavior, 51, 52, 55, 56, 58

D
Domestic violence (DV), 2, 33–42, 51, 75, 78, 80–81, 83–85

I
Interpersonal theory, 6–9, 13
Intimate partners, 2, 33–42, 75, 78, 80–81, 83–85
Intimate partner violence (IPV), 33–35, 41–44, 61, 80, 86

M
Mental health, 2, 4, 6, 8, 9, 11–13, 24–26, 28, 35, 40, 41, 44, 51, 52, 58–67, 76–84, 86
Military, v, vi, 1–13, 19–29, 33–44, 49–67, 75–86
Military culture, 20, 21, 27, 29, 36, 77, 80, 85

S
Self-harm, 2–13, 63, 64, 75–76, 79–82, 84
Sexual, 2, 7, 19, 33, 50, 75
Sexual assault, 19–29, 38, 51, 77, 82, 85
Sexual harassment, 19–29
Sexual hazing, 19–29, 82
Sexual violence, 2, 19–29, 33, 35, 36, 75–78, 80, 82–86
Suicide prevention, 4, 10, 12–13, 82
Suicides, 3–13, 26, 43, 62, 64, 75–76, 79–82, 84, 85
Survivors, 19–29, 76, 77, 80, 82, 83, 85

T
Trauma, 6, 20, 23, 26, 27, 41, 52, 53, 55, 56, 60–62, 64, 65, 76–78, 80, 83, 85

V
Veterans, 2, 4, 5, 8, 10, 11, 13, 22, 26, 28, 35, 36, 41, 49–62, 64–67, 76–79, 81, 83–86
Violence, 1, 3, 20, 33, 49, 75
Violent crimes, 2, 50–53
Violent criminal behavior, 49–67, 75, 78–79, 81, 83–84, 86

M. T. Baker et al., *Violence in the Military*, SpringerBriefs in Psychology,
https://doi.org/10.1007/978-3-031-26883-0

The manufacturer's authorised representative in the EU is Springer Nature Customer Service Centre GmbH, Europaplatz 3, 69115 Heidelberg, Germany. If you have any concerns regarding our products, please contact ProductSafety@springernature.com

Printed and bound by CPI Group (UK) Ltd, Croydon, CR0 4YY
01/10/2026
02225839-0004